EAT
YOURSELF
THIN

LOSE WEIGHT, GAIN ENERGY

E A T
YOURSELF
THIN

LOSE WEIGHT, GAIN ENERGY

Arabella Melville and
Colin Johnson

MICHAEL JOSEPH
LONDON

MICHAEL JOSEPH LTD

Published by the Penguin Group
27 Wrights Lane, London, W8 5TZ, England
Viking Penguin Inc., 40 West 23rd Street, New York, New York 10010,
USA
Penguin Books Australia Ltd, Ringwood, Victoria, Australia
Penguin Books Canada Ltd, 2801 John Street, Markham, Ontario, Canada
L3R 1B4
Penguin Books (NZ) Ltd, 182–190 Wairau Road, Auckland 10, New
Zealand

Penguin Books Ltd, Registered Offices: Harmondsworth, Middlesex,
England

First published 1990
Copyright © Arabella Melville and Colin Johnson, 1990

Made and printed in Great Britain by
Richard Clay Ltd, Bungay, Suffolk
Filmset in Photina by Butler and Tanner Ltd
Frome and London

A CIP catalogue record for this book is available from the British Library.

ISBN 0 7181 3139 8

Contents

Acknowledgements

We are grateful to Maryon Stewart and Alison Bradley of the Women's Nutritional Advisory Service for freely sharing their experience and research results with us; and to our editors Vivien James and Anne Williams for encouragement and direction in the preparation of this book.

Preface

FOR SOME YEARS many athletes, sports and other stars
who need high-power output have been using the techniques of *high-energy physiology*. We have taken the
fundamentals of these techniques and applied them to
everyday life. We have developed a system which will
produce a slim, attractive body shape for anyone, a state
most high-powered performers achieve incidentally.

The results are nothing less than revolutionary.

That claim has been made so often for slimming
methods that it has almost become meaningless. But
this system really is revolutionary because we found
that the *only* way most people can lose fat and stay
slim is *by eating more food*. This is the exact opposite of
conventional slimming wisdom. How does it work?

The way EAT YOURSELF THIN works is very simple. It
involves developing a metabolism that generates more
energy – not just when you're active but all the time.
You actually train your body to burn fat while eating
as much as you want! By eating more nutritious food,
you begin to raise your metabolic rate. You ensure that
your metabolism can turn food into energy by getting
plenty of oxygen into your body. Then you use this
energy in activity to burn fat.

Once you are burning fat, you will need to eat more.
This will raise your metabolic rate higher and your body
will become more efficient at burning fat, which will
enable you to burn more fat. Eventually you will reach
a stable plateau where your food, activity and body
shape are in balance. With this system *you* decide on
the body shape and energy level you want.

EAT YOURSELF THIN tells you how to boost your body
oxygen and nutrient levels to fire your metabolism and
how to use the energy produced – energy that may

surprise you – to burn fat and set yourself up for a thin life. You will learn how to remain slim for life without ever having to go hungry!

High-energy physiology requires the deliberate creation of a high metabolic rate. For athletes this means high performance; for you it will mean that your body uses food to produce energy, energy to repair, maintain, and improve itself – not to produce fat.

A high metabolic rate enables you to live in a vital and enjoyable way. You can only live in this desirable state if your body has enough of the right fuel (food) and is able to use it to produce the effects you want.

To illustrate how this works, we use the comparison of the sleek Harrier jump jet and the 747 jumbo. When the Harrier sits elegantly motionless in the air, its engine works flat out, consuming fuel at an enormous rate. The Harrier has the equivalent to a very high metabolic rate; fuel is consumed even though nothing else appears to happen. By contrast the fat old jumbo jet has a very low metabolic rate. Its engines are on a lean diet and it uses its wings to the full; it will take you and your luggage across the Atlantic at the equivalent of 50 miles per gallon. While this may be very convenient, few of us want the stately bulk of the jolly jumbo. EAT YOURSELF THIN explains how jumbos can turn into Harriers.

You will not have to diet. Diets fail because they create a depressed metabolism, the very opposite of what is required to be naturally thin. The typical dieter, short of nourishment, has low energy, low resistance, low vitality, in fact low everything – except body fat! This is because a depressed metabolic rate is part of a survival routine. The body behaves as if you were starving (which you are) and acts to ensure your survival – by conserving fat. Applying the principles of high-energy physiology to the way you live will produce a metabolism which knows you do not need fat. If you want to be slim and attractive for the rest of your life, without the misery of hunger and constant food obsession, read on and learn how to eat yourself thin.

INTRODUCTION

Get the Best from This Book

A BOOK IS A guide. This book will guide you to a lifestyle that enables you to be permanently slim without going hungry. To get the best from it you will have to be prepared to make the effort that change demands: the guide will show the way but the journey, with its set-backs and final success, is yours. If you are willing, the book will direct you so that your effort is rewarded. If you are enthusiastic, success is almost guaranteed.

We can say this because EATING YOURSELF THIN only requires that you behave in ways which are completely compatible with being a slim, energetic person. At no point will you have to struggle with your real nature or desires; you will not have to suffer or deprive yourself in the pursuit of success. Rather, you will be working with your body and its needs to create fulfillment for yourself.

Obviously we cannot promise an instant trans-formation but we can promise a permanent change in both your body shape and your vitality. By following the strategy in EAT YOURSELF THIN you will be led pro-gressively, step by sure step, away from the lifestyle of a fat person to that of one who is naturally slim.

Although the strategy of EATING YOURSELF THIN is basically simple, some of the details are quite soph-isticated. This is unavoidable since humans are complex, and to further complicate matters we are all subtly different. So while the system will work for practically everyone, particular details will vary from person to person. To assist you there are questionnaires which will ensure you are on the right track for you.

To enable you to get the best out of this book, it has been designed so that as each general principle is

4 EAT YOURSELF THIN

outlined, the relevant details are explained. For easy reference each chapter ends with a summary of the points covered. As you read through, it would be a good idea to keep a note of those which are particularly relevant to you. This will enable you to build up a picture of the changes relevant to you, and also help you monitor your progress.

You will also find 'Action Now' suggestions at the end of each chapter. These will enable you to begin eating yourself thin from the start of the book. The actions we suggest will build up as you work through the book until you reach the 'Action Plans' in Chapter Nine. Here you will be guided onto a specific track suitable for your individual needs, where the actions you have been taking will be complemented by suggestions which will enable you to shed as much fat as you want, reshape your body, and stay slim for life.

So avoid the temptation of turning straight to a chapter that seems to offer an instant answer. A little patience now will be rewarded once you have the full picture of the strategy.

Although you may be convinced that diets do not work, the questionnaire in Chapter Two should not be missed. It will give you an assessment of your current position and, once you have started eating yourself thin, you can return to it to monitor your progress.

If you need convincing, as many accustomed to dieting will, of the soundness of the system, Chapter Three is a must. It explains how hunger and mal-nutrition cause the body to conserve fat – the last thing you want it to do.

From Chapter Four, 'Eat Yourself Thin', you are on your way to success. But to make sure things are going right, there is a questionnaire at the end of Chapter Seven which will allow you to check your metabolic rate.

You will be guided into ways of eating enough good food and we will tell you how to ensure that your metabolism is getting enough oxygen to turn your food into energy. You will then have to make sure you use the energy your body produces in appropriate ways to burn off your unwanted fat.

We will show you how as little as half an hour a day will ensure that fat is never your problem again. Our activitiy reviews will enable you to ease yourself into action with specific guidance which matches the requirements of your individual action plan. And there is a section on trouble-shooting; we all falter or get blocked at times – you should find the key to keeping moving here. Throughout, there is one principle which we stress time and again: the pleasure principle. We want you to enjoy becoming thin and enjoy yourself when you are; sticking to this principle will make sure you do.

Finally you will be led to the last objective in fat loss, a state of balance where food, energy and body shape remain stable at the state you desire.

In following this strategy you will be changing yourself and your way of life. Your lifestyle will move away from that of a fat person to that of someone who is naturally lean. And in so doing you will become slim and stay that way.

A last word. Although this book is primarily aimed at women, its strategy also works for men. Where there are differences between the sexes which are relevant they are noted in the text, and the action plans are suitable for both men and women.

CHAPTER 1

The Diet Nightmare

IMAGINE YOUR PROBLEM is that you are getting too thin.

Imagine having to struggle to eat enough food to avoid becoming gaunt and bony. Impossible unless you are taking some miracle slimming drug? No! This is a problem we have actually experienced and observed in others.

A tennis player we know shocks her boyfriend at the beginning of the season because she eats twice as much as he does. She has to eat over 3,000 calories a day to avoid losing her feminine figure. Our experience is similar. Even spending most of our time as writers, a sedentary occupation, we find we have to eat 2,500 and over 4,000 calories respectively to maintain our fit and non-fat selves. We are not exceptional, nor is our tennis-playing friend. The situation we are asking you to imagine is natural among people who have developed a high metabolic rate.

We are offering you the chance to follow the same course. You do not have to become as physical or energetic as our very shapely tennis player, nor do you have to raise your metabolic rate to the point where you eat as much as we do (the other half of our day is spent on our smallholding) but you *can* get your metabolic rate to the level where you can eat as much as you want, not turn food to fat, and have the sort of energy and vitality you desire, together with a body shape that makes you happy.

A dream too good to be true? If you have spent years trying to diet yourself slim, weight going up and down on the diet seesaw, body turning more flabby and watery every time you gain, it may seem that way. You, and millions like you, are victims of the diet nightmare.

This book is a total rejection of that nightmare. Instead

it offers you lasting success, a way to make your individual dream come true. Your success will be achieved in a completely natural and healthy way, a way that will work for the rest of your life. All you have to do is want the dream to come true – then you can turn it into your reality.

Let us untangle the dream from the nightmare.

Everywhere in the Western world, the majority of people would prefer to be thinner than they are. This is understandable and perfectly natural. Slim people look better and feel better, they tend to be healthier and have more energy, so the dream of a slimmer body, with all its expected benefits, is common. Unfortunately the reality is not.

The dream has turned to nightmare because the means of achieving the dream is itself an illusion. The illusion is that if you eat less, you will get thin. The 95% of dieters who regain weight within a year know diets don't work. Why have we become hooked on them?

The illusion is based on an underestimation of the complexities of the human body. Specifically, it overlooks the many interacting checks and balances of its metabolic cycles. It is assumed that if you eat more than you use, the excess will be stored as fat. This is far from the whole picture of fat metabolism. Behaving as if you can ignore the rest of the picture is both a crucial ingredient of failure and an essential part of the illusion. We will give you the rest of the fat picture, and with it you will be able to see the illusion of simple dieting. The diet nightmare turns eating into horror; the dream allows you to enjoy eating.

The calorie is part of the diet nightmare. More time and energy has probably been expended on calorie counting in the last two decades than was used to create all the wonders of the ancient world. But all this modern effort is wasted.

A calorie is a measurement of heat. To find how many calories there are in a food, it is incinerated under carefully controlled conditions and the heat given off is measured. Thus fatty meats are obviously more calorific than watery vegetables. But the link with fat on the human body is at best tenuous.

To believe in calorie-controlled diets you must also believe the following. That your body can be seen as a simple heat/energy machine; and that calorie input and energy output are all that is involved in fat. Also that you always react in the same way to a given number of calories. That the type of food which produces the calories is irrelevant (a calorie is a calorie . . .) and that we all have identical metabolisms. And so on – the list is almost endless. Since none of these propositions is correct, calorie counting becomes more irrelevant the more you think about it.

To think of food, the most essential pleasure of life, just in terms of calories, and reduce it to meaningless numbers is the stuff of nightmares. Anticipating and consummating its pleasure in any way that takes your fancy is the dream.

Meaningless numbers do not end with calorie counting. Slimmers reduce themselves to numbers. The ritual daily trial by bathroom scale, the fixing of some arbitrary target weight, the flush of guilt and disappointment caused by a few pounds, the illusion of the 'right' weight – all these belong to the nightmare. Your scales cannot tell the difference between a stone of watery flab and a stone of attractive lean tissue.

Just looking at weight is pointless. You are not a sack of potatoes and it is time to stop behaving as if you were; scales have no place in the slim person's dream. Replace your scales with a full-length mirror: what you look like is far more important than what you happen to weigh. If you are very fat or flabby, the prospect of looking at your body may seem off-putting but for your dream to come true, you must face yourself. Focus on your most attractive points, not just the flab; look for the underlying shape that you're going to develop. Why should your body respond positively to you if in return you are going to reject it?

Those who sustain the nightmare encourage the anonymity of numbers, of calories and impersonal figures on scales. Although this may seem to protect you from discomfort or embarrassment, ultimately it works against you because when you fail – as you surely will – the nightmare is strengthened and you are left weak and isolated. If the diet didn't work, it is your fault. The numbers prove that. You had too many calories and you weigh too much.

We are going to tell you how to lose unwanted *fat* and how to reshape your body. To be successful you will have to look at yourself. It is the only way to tell the difference between fat and lean, between shapely muscles and wobbly flab. After all, you do want to see yourself as others see you. . . .

Today almost everyone has heard of lean tissue loss. It is caused by depriving the body of food, as in dieting. If you try to lose weight while failing to meet your body's nutritional requirements, you lose more lean tissue than fat and the faster your weight loss, the greater the proportion of lean you shed. Lean tissues are the muscles and vital organs: the heart (which is both a muscle and the most vital organ), the liver and kidneys. Muscles are essential to the shape of your body as well as its performance. If your vital organs are diminished, so is your vitality, sometimes to a dangerous degree.

The best way to make your dream come true may be to think of yourself not as someone who needs to shed fat, but as someone who is going to become a work of art. Your body is the canvas on which you are going to work, food will be your palette and a new and vital way of life your artistry. You can become your own greatest creative work!

Leave the slimming nightmare behind. Forget the illusion that eating less will make you slim. No more calories and pounds and ounces; they are for technicians and potatoes, not for artists. Dump those scales, they wouldn't know a good thing if it was standing on top of them. And say goodbye to swapping lean tissue for flab on yet another 'miracle' diet; there are no miracles in slimming, only you and what you make of yourself.

Best of all, you can say goodbye to those daylight echoes of the nightmare. In a few short weeks you will look back with disbelief to the time when food was an obsession, when your life was dominated by what you did or did not eat.

We have one more criticism of dieting. Following a diet is a certain way to lose one thing, your self-respect. No diet regime, even if it were correct in its assumptions, can suit every different individual. In trying to make a diet work for you, you lose sight of your unique personal needs and abilities. The inevitable failure makes *you* feel guilty and your desire for success can drive you into obsession. You become one of those callow people who pick fitfully at the best life and the world has to offer. Dieting is such a negative thing.

That is not the way an artist lives. With a high metabolic rate will come energy and vitality, boosting confidence and potential. As you change your body shape you will be experimenting with more food, different types as well as larger quantities, and *enjoying* every mouthful without a twinge of guilt! As your self-artistry becomes more competent you will start to feel much better about yourself, you will like living with the work of art you are creating.

Personal experience, combined with scientific knowledge, are at the roots of our own conviction. We also have a clearer perception of the realities of food, rather than its packaging, and its effects on people. We *know* how dieting can destroy body and spirit, and how eating well and developing a high metabolic rate will transform the way you feel.

Arabella's personal story: a low-energy dieter transformed

Fat – my fat – became an obsession when I was in my teens. I had always been podgy; my only photograph as a child shows a beaming moon-face next to my brother William's small, sharp features. My mother, believing that children should be plump, worried about William; she assured me that dimpled knees were a sign of beauty. Our substantial meals were followed by rich milk puddings, we emptied our plates and accepted seconds. My pocket money went on sweets.

Already well over 9 stone at the age of eleven, I began to feel concerned. I gave up sugar at fourteen and by fifteen I was imitating my mother with periodic bouts of slimming. As boyfriends grew more important, so did anxiety about my size and my slimming efforts intensified. In the sixth form at school I would avoid breakfast, eat cheese with an apple and coffee for lunch, and try to hold out till supper when I'd have as little as I could. The pattern was set for the next decade of semi-starvation.

Ritual weighings confirmed the effects of severe restrictions on food intake. I shrank to a more acceptable size. I took no notice of the fact that I was fainting from hunger: the benefits were worth every sacrifice. But still I found I couldn't wear tight skirts; the bugles at the sides of my thighs created an ugly line of which I was very conscious.

I would have dearly liked to be good at sport – at my school, status lay in team membership – but because I could never run far or fast and my coordination and balance were poor, I soon gave up trying. I was hopeless at games, a useless dancer, a failure at gym. I joined the select group of sport-avoiders. My best friends were plump too.

At university I became more scientific about my dieting. I counted calories religiously and was shocked to discover that the strictest diet produced minimal effects. I lived on a maximum of 1,000 calories a day for month after hungry month. I was chronically cold, tired, short of energy and lacking *joie de vivre*. Even so, I was obviously fatter than most of my fellow students. I would stare disconsolately in the mirror at the dimpled backs of my thighs, wondering why I should be afflicted with such ugliness in an age when Twiggy was the ideal and hemlines revealed all.

Deprivation and despair set off a cycle of alternating crash diets and binges. I would calculate each day's menu carefully and precisely, searching out the most filling and nourishing food I could get for my restricted calorie allowance. My wardrobe contained fat clothes and thin clothes; the latter hardly worn, bought in hope after phases of successful dieting; I would touch them wistfully as my body swelled.

The swings of the diet seesaw grew wilder. I got so fat that the only garment I could get on was a loose kaftan. Then I starved. Eventually I gave up eating completely and felt curiously free, proud of my willpower. Food began to revolt me. I drank black coffee and tossed and turned at night, unable to sleep. My face was thin and haggard but even so, my husband teased me about my persistant thigh bulges and my tummy.

Fortunately, I was too ambitious to allow anorexia to continue indefinitely. Knowing that I could not starve and hope to get a good degree, I consulted a psychiatrist. His advice was simple: start slowly, make yourself eat, first one thing, then another. I acknowledged the need and weaned myself back on to oranges and yoghurt.

I never starved again for more than a day or so: it was too easy and too dangerous. But I continued to diet and still struggled with binges. I was ashamed to be seen eating; it was something I did in secret. Restaurant dinners and meals with friends were torture. There was no joy in food any more; the list of things I wouldn't eat was far too long, the guilt and anxiety too strong.

Controlling my weight remained a problem until my attitudes changed and healthy eating, rather than calorie control, became the priority. Realising I was flabby, I joined a gym. It was the first step towards transformation.

Discovering activities I enjoyed built a positive cycle. I found I loved skiing; not only was it tremendously exhilarating, but it was the first sport where I could match other beginners. I bought sturdy boots so that I could go for long country walks and, well fed at last, I discovered unexpected reserves of stamina. Then a friend taught me how to run, and I learnt to ride a bike with the encouragement of my five-year-old neighbour, Lisa. At the same time, everyday life became more physically demanding as my partner and I renovated a cottage, cultivated a garden and started sawing logs for the fire.

Before long, the transformation was complete. I had no more problems with my weight. I was eating more than ever before, including foods I'd refused for years; yet I was losing those long-hated bulges and dimples. But the most exciting aspect of the whole change was the discovery that I really enjoyed being active. For all those years I'd hated it, felt incompetent and foolish, too ashamed of my body to wear sports clothes and flat shoes – and now I *could* do it, *wanted* to do it, and when I did do it, the fat melted away!

Now, at forty, I'm much fitter, leaner and healthier than I was at fourteen. I can wear tight skirts or nothing at all and look good. I'm not a long-limbed-fashion-model type but nor am I a fatty. I eat up to 3,000 calories a day, ride my bike for pleasure, dance and run when I can, and feel at home in a body in which I can take pride.

I'm not energetic all the time; pressure of work some-times means that I just haven't the opportunity to be as physically active as I would wish. Occasionally I just don't feel like it. Still eating heartily – and I do love my food now the fear of fatness has gone! – I'll slowly put on weight. But when I go back to my healthy, active lifestyle, my body adapts rapidly and any excess fat disappears within days because the energy-generating systems are fully established and my metabolic rate remains high.

What a pity I focussed so firmly on food restriction for all those years; I could have enjoyed my youth so much more. But separating the reality of metabolic effectiveness from the myth of dieting required understanding and experience. I only wish that I had been shown the right direction twenty years earlier!

Summary

The diet nightmare
- Illusion: if you eat less you will get thin
  Fact: 95% of dieters regain weight within a year

- Illusion: counting calories is the way to control your diet
  Fact: calories are meaningless in terms of nutrition and the effects of food on individuals

- *Illusion*: what you weigh is important
  Fact: weight tells you nothing about *quality*; how you look and feel is what matters

The thin dream
- To be able to eat as much as you need
- To have the body shape you desire
- To be vital and energetic

Action now

- *If you have been dieting, gradually let go. Eat a little more each day – add fresh fruit, vegetables, nuts and grains.*
- *Throw away your bathroom scales; put a full-length mirror in the bedroom where you'll see yourself every day.*

CHAPTER 2

Fat or Thin – Which is *Your* Lifestyle?

DOES YOUR WAY of life tend to make you fat or thin? Two essential determinants are your eating habits and the amount of regular activity in your life. The two are closely linked; if your diet is inadequate, you will not have the energy to enjoy activity; and if you are not sufficiently active, your body will not burn off excess fat. Do this questionnaire to find out whether your lifestyle predisposes you to fat. Make a note of your choices and see the next page to assess your score.

A. Eating habits

1. *Do you select your foods primarily for the following?*
   a. Nutritional value
   b. Low calorie content
   c. You choose whatever appeals at the time

2. *Do you deliberately avoid any of the following?*
   (*Select more than one option if appropriate*)
   a. Sugar
   b. Artificial sweeteners
   c. Honey and other unrefined sweeteners
   d. All fat
   e. Animal fat
   f. Meat
   g. Fried food
   h. Synthetic additives
   i. Carbohydrate
   j. Refined carbohydrate

3. *What sort of food do you mainly eat? Pick the feature that is most important in determining your choice.*
   a. Wholefood

    b. Convenience food
    c. Organic food
    d. Ethnic foods, eg Indian, Chinese, Greek

4. *Do you deliberately restrict your calorie intake?*
    a. Yes
    b. No
    c. Sometimes

5. *Do you eat pies, pastries, cakes or biscuits?*
    a. Daily or almost every day
    b. Once or twice a week
    c. Rarely

6. *Do your meals include fresh green vegetables or salads?*
    a. Once or twice every day
    b. Once, most days
    c. Two to four days a week
    d. Once a week or less

7. *Do you eat breakfast?*
    a. Always
    b. Sometimes
    c. Rarely or never

8. *How many meals do you have each day?*
    a. One or two and you try to avoid snacks
    b. Two or three, with occasional snacks
    c. Four or five – you eat whenever you feel peckish
    d. You nibble whenever you feel peckish

9. *Which of the following do you deliberately include in your everyday diet?*
    (*Select more than one option if appropriate.*)
    a. Nuts and seeds
    b. Fish
    c. Celery
    d. Bran
    e. Honey

10. *How many alcoholic or soft drinks do you have in an average week?*
   a. More than 20 standard measures (a measure equals $\frac{1}{2}$pt or a 330 ml can for long drinks; or a single short or a glass of wine for alcoholic drinks)
   b. 10 to 20
   c. Fewer than 10

Scoring
1. a4 b0 c2
2. a2 b2 c1 d −2 e1 f2 g2 h2 i −2 j2
3. a3 b0 c4 d1
4. a0 b4 c2
5. a0 b2 c4
6. a4 b3 c1 d0
7. a4 b2 c0
8. a0 b2 c4 d3
9. a2 b2 c0 d −2 e0
10. a0 b2 c4

Add together your scores for each question. Now use your total to find how you rate ...

45 and above – excellent food choices
You're already well on the way to EATING YOURSELF THIN. If you are over-fat now, your problem is most likely to be due to insufficient activity, or the wrong approach to activity. Go on to the next questionnaire (p 19).

32 to 44 – good but you could do better!
You are aware of the importance of choosing the right food for health but you do not always make the best choices for optimum metabolic efficiency. Are you hung up on old dieting taboos? Do you have a weakness for alcohol, chocolate, chips or some other fat-building food? Make sure you get plenty of the most nutritious foods

you can find – read on to learn which these are – so that you are less likely to be tempted by food that will impair metabolic efficiency.

21 to 31 – you need to be more aware
Either you're not greatly concerned about your food choices, or you've been accepting poor advice. You should change your eating habits so that your body functions better. Start making these changes now, using the questions above and their scores for guidance. The most important rules are these: do not worry about calories; eat whenever you are hungry; and choose natural foods rather than processed, refined products.

20 or fewer – your eating habits are making you fat!
With your choice of food, it's hardly surprising that you have a fat problem. You need to re-think your attitude to food radically; it is probably the single most important determinant of your general health and condition.

To achieve a score as low as this, you are either following discredited dieting rules, in which case you have probably been mystified by your inability to shed fat; or you just don't worry about the quality of your food: you grab whatever is most convenient. Either way, you are likely to be chronically malnourished and suffering a wide range of nutritional deficiencies.

Eating better will demand more time and trouble. If you want to get thin and stay that way, you have no choice about putting that extra effort into a good diet.

B. Activity

When you answer this questionnaire, think carefully about what you have *actually been doing* during the last couple of weeks. It is very easy to kid oneself about activities; most people believe they do more than they actually do. Exaggerating your activity level may make you feel better but you will not solve your fat problem by being dishonest with yourself.

1. *How far do you walk continuously in an average day?*
   a. Less than 1 mile
   b. Between 1 and 2 miles
   c. More than 2 miles

2. *Do you ride a bicycle?*
   a. Yes, every day or most days
   b. Yes, at least once a week
   c. Rarely – less than once a week
   d. No

3. *Which of the following do you do once a week or more often?*
   (Select more than one option if appropriate.)
   a. Any vigorous sport, eg tennis, badminton, squash, football, judo, swimming, rowing
   b. Running
   c. Heavy work, eg digging, shovelling and barrowing
   d. Gym or weight-training
   e. Aerobics, dancing or fencing classes

4. *How often during the past 10 days was your activity sufficiently vigorous to make you sweat for 20 minutes or more?*
   a. 4 or more times
   b. 2 or 3 times
   c. Once
   d. Not at all

5. *How often do you go for long walks (6 miles or more) or long cycle trips (18 miles or more)?*
   a. Usually once a week and more often if possible
   b. At least once a month
   c. Less than once a month but at least 6 times a year
   d. Rarely or not at all

6. *Do you use any home work-out or exercise system (eg Canadian Airforce exercises, aerobics, yoga, dance, trampoline)?*
   a. Yes, three or more times a week
   b. Yes, at least once a week
   c. I have phases of exercise and periods without
   d. I don't use any system of this sort

Scoring

1. a0 b2 c4
2. a4 b2 c1 d0
3. Score 2 for each session of any of these in the last 2 weeks

4. a6 b4 c2 d0
5. a4 b3 c2 d0
6. a4 b3 c2 d0

Over 22 – an active lifestyle

If your activity level is regularly as high as this and you still have more fat than you want, your problem is likely to be with diet. The previous questionnaire should highlight problem areas and this book will give you the precise guidance you need. Alternatively, are you trying to force yourself into a skinny shape that nature never intended for you?

15 to 21 – moderately active

Your activity level could be sufficient to keep you lean – if you get the type and timing of your exercise right and the other factors in your life are in the right balance. The strategy that will unfold as you progress through this book will teach you how to refine your body and choose the best options for maximum effectiveness. You already know that physical activity is good for you but you'll benefit from learning more about it – and from learning about the way the right dietary choices support a lean lifestyle.

6 to 14 – a promising start

When you're in one of the active phases of your life, you probably do quite enough – but because you're either inconsistent or you stop just short of what is necessary to get your metabolism fired up properly, you're not benefiting as much as you could. You've made a good start and you will find it easy to build up when you understand about high-energy eating. If you've been combining a calorie-restricted diet with exercise up till now, you'll have experienced difficulties with increasing your activity level. EATING YOURSELF THIN is the answer you're seeking.

Less than 5
Don't feel that because your activity level puts you in the bottom category, you might as well give up now! The vast flabby majority of British people are right there with you, far too inactive for metabolic efficiency. But you are going to leave them far behind when you discover the joys of a high-energy lifestyle for yourself. Read on – the keys to your success are in this book.

Action Now
Diet
- *Eat whenever you feel hungry and stop counting calories*
- *Give up all sweeteners, both natural and synthetic. When you've progressed through the* Eat Yourself Thin *strategy and raised your metabolic rate so that you're running in a new high-energy balance, you'll be able to enjoy sweet things again – but right now, you should give them up completely. Whenever you want something sweet, go for fresh fruit.*
- *Include 2 oz of fresh, unsalted nuts and seeds (cashews, brazils, walnuts, almonds, sunflower seeds etc – not peanuts) in your daily menu. These provide nutrients that the average British diet lacks – nutrients that are essential to high energy levels.*

Activity
- *Look for opportunities to walk when you would have stayed indoors or taken the car or bus. Walking is the solid bed-rock on which all our energy-generating activities are built; and walking (as we explain later in this book) is the single best form of activity for burning fat. So get those comfortable shoes on and start walking now!*

CHAPTER 3

Hunger Makes You Fat

LET US DEAL with the block that may stop you eating yourself thin: the belief that to be slim you must go hungry. This belief is central to the dieting nightmare and it is based on a misunderstanding of the way the human body actually works.

Conventional slimming assumes that if you reduce your input of food (that is, go hungry), you will lose fat. You do not need to rely on your own experience to see that this belief is ill-founded. National statistics disprove it on a massive scale. As a nation we have, decade by decade, been eating less, yet on average we weigh more – and more of that weight is fat. The input/output equation clearly does not work in the way dieters would like to believe it does.

Look at it another way. In the past twenty years there have been dozens of new and miraculous weight-loss diets. Millions have followed them, many more millions follow various calorie-controlled diets, enormous numbers attend weight-watching groups or combine diet and exercise programmes. All of this effort, pain and perseverance is aimed at one thing – shedding that fat. Yet none of this has provided the long-term success that the majority desire. Why? The answer is dazzlingly simple: because this simple-minded use of the input/output equation is based on false assumptions.

While under some circumstances excess input may be converted to fat, the reverse is not true. Excess fat cannot be shed just by reducing input. The reason why the equation does not work in reverse is because *if input goes down, output cannot go up.*

If the dieting equation were correct any one of the dozens of special diets would have solved the fat problem

for all time. No matter what the publicity, every slimming diet relies on reducing calorie input for its effect.
As we explain in *The Complete Diet Book* (Grafton, 1989),
every bestselling diet *reduces* the amount you eat, even
if it denies the fact. Even those which encourage you to
eat as much as you can actually reduce your input by
limiting your choice of food; even the most ravenous
can only stomach so much pineapple, or whatever, at
one time.

Looked at in practical terms it becomes apparent that
simple reliance on dieting can never achieve all that is
necessary to lose fat permanently. We would go further.
We believe that any way of eating which creates chronic
hunger will tend to make you fat.

How can we justify this belief? It seems to fly in the
face of logic. Think of those pictures of hungry people
in the Third World – they are certainly not fat. But we
must distinguish clearly between hunger and starvation.
People who starve lose weight, both fat and lean tissue.
Eventually they die, either when they are too weak to
resist attack by pathogens or when a vital part of the
self-consuming body fails.

Hunger occurs when you do not get enough of all or
some of the things your body needs for its maintenance.
Its cause can vary from simply not having enough to
eat, to the complex malnourishment seen in the rich
countries of the Western world. In the latter, people may
stuff themselves to bursting point on a regular basis but
still experience hunger because the sort of food they eat
does not contain the right balance of nutrients to meet
their needs. Hunger is a message from your body, telling
you to seek more or different food.

Dieting is self-imposed hunger. Diet writers devote so
much effort to explaining that you *won't* feel hungry, or
that what you feel is *not* hunger (or not *real* hunger)
that you can be sure that you will, and it is. Because of
the wide range of differences in individual nutritional
needs, a low-calorie diet is also likely to be self-imposed
malnourishment.

One type of dietary system, the Very Low Calorie Diet (VLCD), is based on formula products which are said to meet all nutritional needs. But while these are standard products, their customers are not, and their individual nutritional needs cannot be met by any formula. These diets, acclaimed as the ultimate route to slimness, seem rather to combine the worst aspects of food restriction: maximum lean tissue loss, maximum metabolic depression and maximum fat recuperation after the diet. No wonder many governments and medical bodies have issued warnings against them.

So how does hunger make you fat? When you go hungry, whether through a slimming diet or malnourishment, you are giving your body an unambiguous message: PREPARE FOR FAMINE.

The message can take many forms. You may not be getting enough of the many micronutrients, minerals and trace elements which are essential for healthy functioning. You may be vitamin deficient or you could be eating an imbalance of carbohydrates, proteins and fats. If you eat modern processed convenience foods, you probably have deficiences at every level. Whatever your particular dietary deprivation, your metabolism will register the shortage and it is likely to react by sending your brain the message 'eat more', making you feel hungry.

If you are one of the 60% who have been dieting to lose weight, this hunger will be familiar. Caught in the turmoil of the dietary nightmare, you will have tried to resist it as a devilish temptation sent to test your resolve. Most diets warn of the need for character and discipline for just such occasions. Now, they say, is the time to harden your resolve, resist the biscuit, grin and bear it, and do all the other things that are characteristic of dieters.

But when you awaken to reality, you will understand the importance of the message, if not its precise meaning. Hunger may be your body saying it needs more iron, or vitamin C, or selenium so that your immune system can protect you from an infection, or that it needs more protein for repairs, or carbohydrate to fuel itself, or any of many substances which carry out the complex functions that make up your life.

For some people, hunger and fat deposition are both symptoms of chronic malnourishment. Unable to maintain a proper metabolic balance because of deficiencies of essential nutrients such as chromium, the malnourished person's blood sugar swings wildly up and down, causing fat deposition as it rises, and hunger as it falls.

Going hungry will not persuade your body to find the things it needs from fat. Nothing can, because it is just not possible. Fat is reused by the body, *but it can only be used to produce energy*, and this only under certain circumstances (which we shall explain in detail in the next chapter). The only way to get the balance of nutrients your body needs is to eat them.

Hunger can have a limited positive effect, but only if you are well nourished. Fasting for a day or so, as recommended in many ancient health regimes and religions, can be beneficial. It allows all your systems to refresh and re-balance themselves. But the most important part of the process is listening to the needs of your body, so that after fasting you eat the foods your body needs and the balance achieved is maintained at a high level of metabolic activity. During brief periods of fasting weight is lost, but as with diets most of the loss will be water, and again as with diets, this will be quickly replaced.

A brief episode of fasting is not the same as the protracted hunger of the dieter. Under a regime of constant hunger the body will recognise famine and set in train a survival routine. First, your metabolic rate will decline. This means that resources are rationed, energy and material is directed towards essential functions. Energy for frivolous activity is cut down. Under these conditions everything becomes an effort and you tend to lose interest in things in general. Life is reduced as far as possible to a basic routine, which is what survival is about. While you exist in this lack-lustre state, *any* food you eat will be marked for priority use – to be stored as fat!

For all your body knows, things may be going to get worse. From a survival point of view this is the only safe assumption. So the manufacture and conservation of fat becomes the order of the day, and will remain so as long as you remain hungry.

The longer you inflict hunger on yourself the worse things will get. Your metabolic rate will fall lower and your body will shed lean tissue. You will lose weight, but most of this will not be fat; you will shed pounds from your muscles and vital organs. To your body this makes survival sense; after all you don't need muscles when you haven't got the energy (food) to use them, and a shut down metabolism does not require great cardiac capacity or a vigorous liver and efficient kidneys. Reducing lean tissue saves on running costs and cuts back repair and maintenance bills because lean tissue is very much more metabolically active than fat and it requires more food to maintain it.

Fat will be saved to the last because when you are (literally) exhausted it will provide the energy to keep the vital spark of life burning, in the hope of an end to famine. The more often you go into the diet/hunger routine, the quicker your body will respond by conserving fat. This is the mechanism of the diet seesaw; every time your weight goes down, your fat goes up – and when your weight comes up again, fat comes up faster than lean tissue. Some experts believe lean tissue loss can take years to be made up, and then only with care and persistence. Dieting not only makes you fat, it should be the subject of government health warnings.

Next time you see one of those enviably slim people, look again more closely. Are they on this hopeless path? Do their pinched and brittle features display the delicate destruction they are imposing on themselves, or are they vitally alive, and robust enough to cope with everything life has to offer? Are they victims of the nightmare, or people for whom the dream has come true?

Hunger makes you fat. Persisting with hunger to lose weight destroys the very parts of your body, not to mention your spirit, upon which an enjoyable, healthy and energetic life depends. Lest you be left in any doubt, hunger has no intrinsic virtue; those famine victims on your TV screen, all skin and bone, their fat consumed, die unless they are very lucky and receive dedicated individual care for a long time. That is the true tragedy of their situation.

In those countries where famine is a thing of the past, the tragedy is of a different kind. We noted earlier that hunger can be caused by the lack of vital micronutrients in food. Under these circumstances people can eat normal quantities and, although they may not be aware of hunger, still provoke their bodies into fat conservation routines; their metabolic rates fall so that fat accumulates. This may be the startling reason why we are eating less but weighing more.

The very nature of food has changed dramatically in the last few decades. Yes, everyone over a certain age believes things were better *then*, at some time in the past when they were young and carefree, but with food it is a matter of fact. We used to eat naturally produced plants and animals, grown on farms which were self-sufficient, except for a few specialist items supplied by small-scale rural industries. What went on your plate was wholesome, or if not it was *naturally* bad and usually recognisable as such.

In the wake of the Second World War, when the population of Britain was shown to be dependent on many other parts of the world for its food, policy changed. The pressure to produce more, which has culminated in our contribution to the EEC food mountains, was instigated.

The only way Britain could produce more food was by radical change in every area of agriculture. The natural cycles of fertility were broken, livestock no longer interacted with grain and vegetable crops in ways which sustained the soil. At an ever increasing rate farmers were led away from self-sufficiency and on to the high-tech chemical treadmill. Agriculture became chemiculture; and while the quantity of food produced has gone up, its quality has suffered disasterously, and many people are showing the effects of this deterioration in the nutritional value of their food by becoming fat.

High crop yields are achieved by a high level of use of chemical fertilisers made of three basic plant foods, nitrogen, potassium, and phosphate or NPK. This has had profound effects on the quality of our food. Successive crops take a wide range of minerals out of the soil but when only three chemicals are put back, the soil becomes exhausted, incapable of producing nutrient-rich crops. Most of the micronutrients which we should get from the soil via our food have been extracted *and not replaced*. The situation is made worse by the fact that heavy applications of NPK fertilisers reduce the availability to plants of essential minerals like magnesium, even when they are still present in the soil.

Food processing, preservation and cooking strips yet more nutritional value from the food. On top of that, our food choices may be ill-judged or we may eat too little good food. Add to this our increased need for micronutrients to cope with a polluted environment and you have a recipe for disaster.

Thus we experience malnutrition amid apparent plenty, and hunger among populations which appear well fed. The famine response of fat conservation is triggered among more people as it becomes increasingly impossible to meet all our bodily needs from the products of the modern food industry. We simply cannot eat enough modern food to provide adequate nutrition – because the nutrients we need are not there.

The modern food industry helps you get fat in another way. Just as we put on more fat through malnourishment, whether self-imposed or from dietary inadequacies, so do the animals which we eat. Today's inactive farm animals are encouraged to put on 'weight' with regular doses of antibiotics and growth hormones, so we are fed more fat, which helps us make more fat. It may not appear on our plate directly; the food processing industry will take animal fats away from the meat and smuggle them into your food in many disguises. Everything from biscuits to ice cream contains as much fat as it can carry.

Dieters, with their self-imposed and destructive hunger, form the hard core of an increasingly hungry population. Even those who would never consider a diet are likely to suffer nutrient deprivation if they eat normal British food. We suffer junk food and the empty calorie because that is what the chemiculture food industry delivers.

Hunger makes you fat. Dieters carry more fat than would be possible if their diets really worked. Ordinary people are eating less, yet getting fatter decade by decade. It is a situation that could provoke despair for anyone who cares and really wants to be slim.

Although it may seem as if the whole world is conspiring to make you fat – and in many ways it is – there is a way out. It is quite possible to avoid hunger and all its pitfalls. It is quite possible to be naturally slim and healthy. It is quite possible to eat as much as you want, without suffering the famine/fat reaction. It is quite possible for you to be slim. But you need nothing less than a revolution to achieve it. We will tell you how it works.

Summary

- When you are hungry or malnourished, your body acts to conserve fat.
- When your body is trying to conserve its fat it is reluctant to put it to its natural use – producing energy.
- If your food input goes down, your energy output will go down too.
- When you remain hungry, your body consumes its own lean tissue and your metabolic rate falls.

● Modern processed food leads to malnourishment because it does not contain all the nutrients we need for good health.

Action Now

○ *Check over the food you've been eating recently. How much of it was fresh, how much processed and stripped of nutrients? Gradually try changing to wholefoods – wholemeal bread, wholemeal flour, brown rice, whole grain cereals, organically produced if available. Study labels carefully to see precisely what you're buying.*

CHAPTER 4

Eat Yourself Thin

SHEDDING FAT BECOMES automatic when you start to live in a way that makes excess fat a disadvantage to your body.

In this chapter we shall explain not only how to make fat something your body treats as a disadvantage, but also how to live in a way which makes fat irrelevant, so that it will no longer be your problem.

Hunger makes fat an advantage. Just as poorer people believe they have to save money, so a deprived body believes it has to conserve energy. The result is a low metabolic rate and a body which stores fat. Richer people tend not to save. They may have something stashed away because they don't know what to do with it, but that is different. They don't save because they know there is plenty more where their first lot of money came from. Slim people tend not to accumulate fat, although if they *grossly* overeat they may stash the excess away as fat which they can easily lose again. They tend not to accumulate fat because their body sees no reason to do so.

If you have a fat problem the first thing you must do is stop thinking and behaving like a fat person! To be thin you must think and behave like a thin person.

Ah, if only I were thin, you will say, *then* I could live like a thin person. The old chicken and egg problem. Let's be realistic, you can only start from where you are, which we assume is someone with a fat problem. By avoiding hunger (fat person behaviour) you will be taking one step; by EATING YOURSELF THIN (thin-person behaviour) you will almost have arrived. The great advantage of EATING YOURSELF THIN, as we shall explain, is that from the very start you behave as you are going to go on behaving indefinitely. There is no suffering to be endured for some over-the-rainbow illusion. You simply start to behave in the way you will when you are thin, *and doing this helps make you thin.*

The Eat Yourself Thin Strategy

We shall apply the lessons of *high-energy physiology* used by athletes and high-energy performers to your every-day situation. You don't have to become an athlete, although you will become more energetic and competent. Neither will you have to go in for the sort of demanding training routines athletes do, although you will naturally be more active.

Your first objective will be to raise your metabolic rate.

What exactly does that mean? Your metabolism is that complex of chemical (more correctly electro-chemical) processes by which your body maintains all your life processes. Your metabolism is the way you convert food to substances your body needs; it is the way those substances are used, with oxygen from the air, to produce energy; it is the way each part of your being gets the fuels and materials it needs for the multitude of tasks each has to carry out. To be thin, you need to speed those processes up.

As we have seen, dieting and hunger do the very opposite: they slow your metabolism down. To make your metabolism run faster, you need fuel. Remember, diets fail to make you thin because your metabolism cannot run on fat. You have to *eat* to fuel your metabolism – it will not run on thin air either!

The logic is unassailable. Think of that other thing you wish would run on air, your car. Engine turning over, stationary, in neutral. If you try to pull away without putting your foot on the accelerator and giving the engine (the car's metabolism) more fuel, it will stall. So will you.

Even more than your car, you are dependent on the

quality of the fuel you get. The food you eat may be equivalent to one-star, highly polluted junk. To get your metabolism running fast and smoothly, you want the equivalent of five-star, lead-free: the best. More on this later. Once you have raised your metabolic rate you will have initiated a positive cycle.

Your second objective is to use your increased metabolic rate to burn body fat. Your increased metabolic rate will enable you to use more energy, and burning fat will provide that energy. Remember, providing energy is all that fat will do. If you eat more, your metabolism will be able to cope with burning even more fat – and you will be EATING YOURSELF THIN!

Scientists have repeatedly demonstrated that eating more food produces a rise in metabolic rate, even in the absence of any other lifestyle change. Their name for this phenomenon is *luxus consumption*. For you it means time to slip into gear, put your foot down, and go.

There is a limit to EATING YOURSELF THIN at this level. You may not be able to cope with the energy potentially available to you. You will either have to slow the process down, or use more of that energy. The questionnaires on pages 82 and 103 in the book will guide you on to the best track to ensure that you lose fat in the best possible way. For now, let's assume that your new-found energy and the good feeling that being well fed is giving you are carrying you forward. What happens next?

The positive cycle continues!

Your next objective is to use the energy produced by burning fat to burn more fat. Read that again. It is so simple, isn't it? This is why EAT YOURSELF THIN is a real revolution in fat loss. As you produce more energy you will become more active and your activities will be types that will burn fat, reshape your body, and increase your metabolic rate still further. Conventional hunger-inducing metabolism-lowering, depressing diets just expect fat to evaporate passively, and we all know it does not. The negative cycle those regimes encourage makes fat conservation inevitable. EATING YOURSELF THIN is the exact opposite, a positive cycle that makes shedding fat automatic because you will be living in a way which makes fat a disadvantage to your body.

And what happens when the fat is gone?

You could end up with the problem we described in Chapter One. You could be like our tennis-playing friend, having to eat a lot of food just to keep your weight stable, with hardly any fat in sight. The food you eat then will be used for energy and maintenance, *not* for conservation as fat. When you have achieved this, your slim dream will have come true. You will be living, thinking, and looking like a thin person – and wondering why you wasted all those years on counter-productive diets.

It would be irresponsible to claim that EATING YOURSELF THIN will get rid of *all* your fat. Oh, you will become slim, and have a better shape than you thought possible. Your body will be lean and eager, ready to go, and full of energy, but you will still carry some fat. It is part of being healthy; even healthy men carry some fat and women should have more fat than men.

Essential Functions of Fat

Now you know you are going to be slim it would be a good idea to get a realistic perspective of fat. Physiologically, fat is essential to your body. Nerve cells and brain tissue are made of fat, as are the membranes which separate every cell and organ from each other. So life would be impossible without a proportion of fat; it is everywhere in various amounts; even the leanest tissue has some fat.

Of more interest is the fat specifically associated with the female body shape. According to conventional wisdom, fat is fat is fat. Not so. Female body fat has four distinct functions and ignoring the very different things which fat does for your body can lead to failure, no matter how you try to slim.

The four functions of fat, some of which obviously only apply to women, are these. 1) sexual shaping, 2) insulation, 3) energy storage, 4) toxin storage. Although overlapping in some areas, these functions fulfil very different needs. Unless these needs and their relevance to your situation are understood, you could be working against yourself when you try to reduce the amount of fat you are carrying. Let us look briefly at each of these functions of fat.

1. Sexual shaping

The slimming culture tends to overlook the fact that it is body fat which gives women their sexually attractive shape. The changes that take place in the shape of young girls' bodies as they approach maturity, the accumulation of fat in the 'right' places, principally the breasts and buttocks, send sexual signals. To the male the signals mean, 'I am mature and ready to be approached.' To other females they say, 'I am mature and should be treated as an equal.' For parents the signal is: 'I am at a very awkward age.' Without the shaping provided by this fat the desirable feminine shape is lost.

2. Insulation

We live in the temperate zone of the world, far from the sub-tropical climate where humans evolved. Temperate zone people have adapted to cope with the variable and fickle climate by being able to put fat on very quickly when food is plentiful and the weather turns chilly, losing it slowly and cautiously as needed or when summer returns.

With modern compensations, such as central heating and warm transport, this adaptation need not be used. Most people who trust their bodies will find a little fat going on in the winter and coming off in the spring as part of the natural annual cycle. If your metabolism is not depressed, the slight amount of winter fat will be available for energy should you either become cold or catch one. In the former case it will heat you to keep you warm, in the latter it will contribute to raising your temperature to kill the viruses.

3. Energy storage

Everyone knows that we store excess food as fat. The slimming industry behaves as if this were the only function of fat; it is with this limited view of fat that the slimming industry attempts, and fails, to deal with the problem.

In women of reproductive years, the body will consider a store of fat desirable. This will be over and above that required for shaping and heat insulation. There is an inescapable survival logic behind this tendency: having become shapely and attractive, in the nature of things women then become pregnant. Their bodies want to ensure that there are enough reserves to keep mother and baby well through nine months of pregnancy and perhaps a year of breastfeeding.

While women are sexually active their bodies will push for a little extra fat. However, since an outbreak of love and/or lust generally causes fat to melt away because a heightened emotional state speeds up the metabolism, the body may over-compensate once desire is attained or fulfilled, and once more exert its desire for a reserve of fat. (The 'you are taking me for granted and letting yourself go' phase.)

So any woman experiencing a normal sex and love life will find her emotions having what may appear to be a contrary effect on her body. And if your emotional life is in turmoil and you turn to food for comfort ... When you understand why your metabolism is reacting as it is, it is easier to work *with* your body to achieve a satisfactory compromise. Slimmers do the opposite; they attempt to batter their bodies into submission. Either their body wins or they lose. There is never a happy outcome to such self-destructive wars.

4. Toxin storage

Many of the substances in our environment are poisonous, and the majority of these toxins can be dissolved in fat. If your body cannot metabolise these substances and get rid of them, they can get stored in fat. The body may manufacture fat especially for storage because fat is relatively metabolically inactive and therefore the safest place for dangerous substances. Once toxins have been stored in this way, the body can be very loathe to face them again. The fat becomes persistent, locked onto the bodies of toxin victims. Nor does it end there; once the metabolism has learned to dump things it does not like into fat, it tends to do the same thing with a wider range of substances.

The toxic substances which cause this reaction in many people cannot be simply identified. We face the problem of individual variability among people and their individual reactions to the tens of thousands of artificial chemicals which now circulate in every part of our environment. Many of these substances end up inside us, and if your personal metabolic make-up cannot cope, it protects you by dumping the substance in fat.

If your problem is persistent fat retention caused by toxins, this will rapidly become apparent and we will direct you to further help. It is important that you do not discount the possibility, particularly if you are carrying a lot of fat. The only way you will be able to shed fat successfully is by attending to any factors which may be producing persistent fat. The EAT YOURSELF THIN strategy may allow you to shed persistent fat, but for some individuals it may not be enough. If you do need special help, do not despair! There is an answer and we can help you find it.

Eat Yourself Thin – the Method

For everyone, the statement at the beginning of this chapter – that shedding fat becomes automatic when you start to live in a way that makes fat a disadvantage to your body – remains true. It is important to remember that the essence of your success is to think and behave like a thin person, no matter what you are now. That way you will become what you want to be, rather than remain as you are.

We have outlined the strategy of EATING YOURSELF THIN and described the nature of the fat you are going to lose. Finally in this chapter we will explain the method which, with the application of your own personal artistry, will enable you to eat yourself thin.

1. You are going to eat more good food! We will give you guidance on specific foods which will provide the nutrients necessary to raise your metabolic level. For some this change may be enough to start the fat moving! Some of those who continue to hang on to those evil old scales may notice an increase in weight at this stage. Do not panic! Soon you will see changes reflected in your mirror that make you forget numbers and weights.

2. We will encourage you to use your increasing metabolic capacity to burn fat through activity. This will involve eating more, on a balanced high-energy diet. Although you will not be bothering with scales any more, your weight will stabilise, and best of all, your body will start to refine itself. Fat will begin to move out, and good lean tissue to move in. You will be on your way.

3. You will be experiencing a *natural* increase in energy. This may be a unique experience for many; we will direct you so that you can use your increased energy to burn more fat, and produce more energy! By this time you should be eating as much as you want.

4. We will show you how to get your body into balance, so that you can use the energy your fat is producing constructively, and maintain yourself as a *naturally* slim person for the rest of your life. That is what EAT YOURSELF THIN is all about.

Summary

- To become thin you must think and behave like a thin person.

Here's How:

1. Raise your metabolic rate by eating more good food.
2. Use your increased metabolic capacity to burn fat.
3. Live in a way that makes fat a disadvantage to your body.

Action Now

○ *Make sure you do not go hungry. Thin people see no virtue in depriving themselves of food when their bodies need it.*

CHAPTER 5

Use Food to Burn Fat

YOU BECOME THIN and stay that way by persuading your body to produce as much energy as it can, using all the available fuel. If you have excess fat you obviously want to use this as much as possible. In this chapter we will explain why you need to eat enough food to burn fat, and why the more you eat, the more fat you are capable of burning.

First, you have to raise your metabolic rate. It does not matter how high or low it is now; any increase in metabolic rate will help you shed fat. Burning fat will release energy. To continue the process so that you become as thin as you want, you have to use that energy. Then food will be burning fat, and you will be thin.

To achieve this, once more we have adapted the lessons of *high-energy physiology* so that you can train your body not to conserve fat. This means you need to have a body which is inefficient in food terms. A typical dieter has very efficient food usage, producing enough energy to live and to conserve fat. The thin person is the very opposite; food flows in and energy bubbles out, available for everything except making fat.

The food use of dieters, athletes, and thin people can be compared thus: dieters have low input, low metabolic rate, and low output; athletes have high input, high metabolic rate, and high (but very controlled) output; naturally thin people have high input, high metabolic rate, and high output. All the training that athletes do is to enable them to control their very high outputs. Steve Cram does not run everywhere, but when he does run he wants maximum output. You want enough energy to enjoy life and that means just letting it bubble over most of the time. So you will *not* have to train like an athlete (although you can if you want) but you will have to get your muscles into good condition.

The reason for this is quite simple. Your muscles are the place where fat is burned.

Fat has to be re-metabolised by the body. It has to be burned by eating enough food to keep the metabolic fires alight. If you don't eat enough food to burn your fat, your body will use its own lean tissue for energy. This is how dieters lose weight but keep their fat, getting slim for a short time but ending up shapeless. Dieters don't so much lose fat as lose their capacity for living with vitality.

Although traditionally ladies used to have an aversion to muscles and things muscular, most now accept that they underwrite the shape of our bodies. Shed surplus fat, and the shape which remains is that provided by your muscles. So you need good muscle tone both to enable you to burn fat and also to give attractive shape to what will be revealed once the fat is gone.

It you are a typical over-fat person the thought of using your body may be alarming. You *know* it is uncomfortable, if not painful, to exert yourself. You *know* activity is not a source of pleasure. Of course, this is true for fat people. Your body will make every effort to stop you using its precious fat stores. It will make your muscles ache, make you breathless, give you a headache, and so on. But when your body is convinced it does not need to conserve fat or energy, your experience will be totally, almost unbelievably, different. No more on this now, we just ask you to take it on trust. When you change your lifestyle to that of a thin person, in the way we shall explain later, you will feel one bad emotion – regret. Regret that your life had previously lacked this exhilaration!

Athletes are the experts at high-energy living. They can eat enormous quantities of food, yet they stay very lean. Distance runners face the opposite problem from slimmers; they have to struggle to get enough food into

themselves for the energy they require, and they don't
get fat because fat is of no advantage to their bodies. For
ordinary people who maintain a high metabolic level,
and avoid junk foods and sweets, the sheer bulk of food
they consume can be formidable. This is what happens
when food and energy are unrestricted; when both are
in free-flow the result is an unrestricted and pleasurable
lifestyle.

Your Metabolism and Energy

How do we achieve this, how does your metabolism
actually work to produce energy? Let us start with the
larger picture. Energy is stored at a variety of sites in
the body, principally in the muscles, the liver, and of
course in fat depots. To use this energy to burn the
body's fuel, we use oxygen. This is circulated around
the body from the lungs in blood, which depends on a
healthy heart to move it around effectively. It is our
consumption of oxygen that scientists measure when
assessing metabolic rates. A person with a high metabolic rate will use much more oxygen, and thus will
produce much more energy, than someone with a low
metabolism.

Every cell in the body needs energy, both to maintain
itself and to fulfil its function within the whole. Inside
each cell are specialised energy production units called
mitochondria. These are tiny complex biochemical
power stations which can burn both carbohydrates and
fat to generate heat and to power the equally complex
biochemical and physiological systems of the body.
Muscle cells which produce sustained energy contain
large numbers of big mitochondria. Mitochondria pro-
liferate and develop to meet the demands put on muscles,
which is why activity – whether the specialised training
of the athlete or the enjoyable energy use of the thin
person – is essential. *The more mitochondria you have in
your cells, the more fat you can use up.*

The most important food fuel for energy production is

carbohydrate. This comes from those foods traditionally restricted to dieters: starches and sugars. These are broken down by digestion and rebuilt by the metabolism to form long-chain molecules of glycogen. These are stored in muscles, ready for immediate use, and in the liver which acts as a glycogen reservoir.

Poor dieters! If they live on a low-carbohydrate diet, even for a few days, their glycogen stores will be depleted. Lacking the necessary fuel, their muscles work sluggishly, tire easily, and recover from exertion very slowly. They become inactive and get fatter. Even if your diet is high in carbohydrate, you can still run short of glycogen if you exercise long and hard enough. This is what happens to marathon runners when they 'hit the wall'; there is just no glycogen left. The same thing happens to dieters who go in for aerobics; they do not have enough energy reserves to benefit from the activity, so it becomes a painful, self-defeating exercise.

Vigorous activity always requires glycogen. But this is not the only fuel your muscles will use – they also burn fat. However, muscles prefer glycogen. They cannot use fat as readily, and they cannot burn fat without glycogen. This is where the dieter's lean tissue goes; it is converted to glycogen and consumed in preference to fat. Biochemists used to say 'fat burns in the flame of carbohydrate', and while this is not a precise description, it is a good enough approximation. If your metabolism is fired up and fuelled with food, you will burn fat.

No matter how fit you are, it is difficult to persuade your muscles to work with a ratio of glycogen to fat of less than 1:1 so you must always have plenty of glycogen available to allow you to burn fat. The longer your exercise session continues, the higher the proportion of fat you can burn but your body will not actually be burning more fat than glycogen until you've been at it for over four hours! If you are fit and walk for eight hours, you may be able to push the proportion of fat used as high as 90% – but you will have used up a lot of glycogen getting to this point.

Usually muscles use far more glycogen than fat but the ratio improves with gentle, persistent training. The essential thing is to make sure you eat enough food to provide the carbohydrate which keeps your glycogen levels up, to maximise the fat-burning potential of your muscles.

Many people who try to lose fat by exercise, or by a combination of diet and exercise, fail because they do not understand the metabolic processes involved. When we first start to exercise, our muscles run entirely on their local stores of glycogen. There is a delay before any fat is mobilised or more glycogen released from the liver. This is why athletes warm up; they want those deeper reserves on-stream. Most slimmers do not continue for long enough to break through the warm-up barrier; they may start enthusiastically but quickly give up, perhaps when their depleted glycogen stores begin to run out. If they never exercise for more than a few minutes, their fat reserves won't get touched. And the more often this happens, the more the body comes to rely on muscle glycogen and the less readily it will mobilise fat.

It will come as no surprise that the diet industry quotes research which reveals that fat people's muscles do not burn fat. This research just reports a self-per-petuating-situation; if fat people had taken sufficient action to keep their muscle fuelling systems working as they should, they would not have grown fat and inert!

If you are fat, do not despair. This does not mean that your muscles cannot burn fat, merely that they need re-training – a little gentle persuasion to get them going in the right direction. We will explain how to do it later, on p 119.

After perhaps 10 minutes of moderate exercise, fat becomes an increasingly important source of fuel. The longer the activity continues, the larger the contribution made by fat. One benefit of regular activity (thin-person behaviour) is that the switch from pure glycogen to a mixture of glycogen and fat occurs earlier in more active people. This makes good sense in terms of the body's economy because fat stores contain sufficient energy for many days of continuous activity, but using them requires that complex biochemical systems come into action. This is another difference between EATING YOURSELF THIN and dieting: you are working with your body in using its systems, not against it by suppressing them.

For these processes to work smoothly, all the fuel, oxygen and other needs of the biochemical reactions in each cell must be available in abundant quantities. Making sure there is enough fuel, derived of course from food, is the rationale behind EAT YOURSELF THIN; your body will not work properly without it! Your food must be plentiful, high quality and nutritious; for an artist creating a thing of beauty, only the best materials are good enough. The types of food we recommend will provide the micronutrients so necessary for peak metabolic effectiveness.

Getting enough oxygen is also essential. Without it, your muscles cannot work properly and will tire quickly. If your muscles get less oxygen than they need, you suffer painful cramping sensations when you try to use them. To get all the oxygen you need for activity, you have to develop a healthy heart and lungs – which is another benefit of regular progressive exercise!

There are two potential problems for habitual dieters and people with a lot of fat. First, their hearts may be as under-used as the other muscles of their bodies, and therefore not capable of delivering enough oxygen-rich blood to their muscles. Second, many slimmers smoke. They often do this to suppress appetite and cope with the torment of hunger – but with the EAT YOURSELF THIN system this is not only unnecessary, it's counter-productive! Smoking constricts the blood vessels that feed the muscles and the heart, restricting the flow of blood. This means that smokers are more likely to suffer heart disease and blood vessel problems of all types and it's one of the reasons they find activity difficult.

Later we will give guidance on activities to improve

the oxygenation of the body. Do not worry if at present you are still inactive and lacking in energy. Anyone can get fit enough to shed fat – you just have to start behaving like a thin person!

In improving your oxygen supply, you will also be improving the delivery of fuel and micronutrients. This will happen automatically because the circulating blood delivers and collects everything around your body. So building up your heart's capacity to move more oxygen to burn more fat will also enable your system to move more fuel to your muscles.

Turning Food Into Fuel

We keep talking about food and fuel; the process by which one is converted into the other is worth considering. When we eat food, each stage of the process involves a progressive reduction from what the food was, into the substances we need. These biochemical changes depend on a wide variety of enzyme systems, which in turn are sustained by micronutrients derived from food.

Appetite, in its many variations, is derived from internally generated feelings of hunger combined with visual and odour stimulation, through to the satisfaction of taste and yearnings, and is designed to ensure that we eat what our bodies need. All the messages from the eyes, nose, mouth and emotions are important communications from our bodies, guiding us to fulfilment of our personal needs. Overriding the demands of your appetite usually means that you are depriving your body of something it needs.

Once the digestive system has broken food down sufficiently, it is converted in the liver into substances the body can use. The liver is an organ of awe-inspiring complexity, the industrial centre of the body. It is made up of many similar lobules, each of which processes incoming material, stores nutrients, and sends out things the body needs or despatches them as waste. The liver knows what is needed because it is connected to every other part of the body; it performs over twenty major metabolic functions, including controlling body temperature, using fat reserves to raise it when necessary. The liver is a major energy and nutrient store, providing fuel when the muscles have used up their immediate reserves and turning on a flush of energy in emergencies. The exhausted walker can suddenly sprint to avoid a bull because the liver discharges glycogen under the stimulation of adrenalin.

The liver will order fat out of store when necessary, for conversion into energy. But this will only happen if there is enough other fuel (notably glycogen) and oxygen in the system to allow the fat to be used.

Releasing fat from storage for re-metabolism depends on the effectiveness of the enzyme systems involved. The crucial enzymes for fat release are called lipoprotein lipases (LPLs). Both the quantity and effectiveness of LPLs varies with the degree to which the body has experienced a need for them. If you draw on your fat stores frequently, you will have higher LPL activity than if you do not. Athletes have much higher LPL activity than sedentary people and women have higher LPL activity than men.

This last fact is important. It makes sense, since women are meant to have larger stores of fat. Women are designed for long-haul endurance; they could leave most men far behind if the race lasted long enough. This means that every woman has the potential for substantially greater use of fat – an advantage the EAT YOURSELF THIN system, with its adaptation of high-energy physiology, exploits to the full.

Once your metabolism learns a preferred way of coping with a situation, it tends to hang on to it. In the case of people who are generally short of food or metabolic capacity, the body learns to conserve fat. In the case of people who get plenty of good food, the liver and metabolism learn that there is no need for fat, so it gets used as often as possible. In changing your behaviour from that of a fat person to a thin person, you will change the way your body works in relation to your fat; your LPL capacity will increase along with the capacity of all the other enzyme systems involved in fat metabolism.

Your Liver and Waste Disposal

One aspect of liver function which is particularly important for anyone losing fat is the metabolism of waste products. The liver deals with all the waste produced by the metabolic processes in the body. This may include debris from battles between the immune system and invading viruses and bacteria, and all the day-to-day clearing up. By-products of activity in the muscles are re-metabolised in the liver. Obviously, a depressed metabolism will not be able to cope with as much waste as a fast-running metabolism. Not only does this mean that less fat can be burned, it also accounts for some of the pain and aches that cause people with depressed metabolisms to dislike activity. The liver puts a double bind on them; first it denies them fuel because they are not eating enough; then it restricts the waste disposal capacity to make activity unpleasant so that fat can be conserved – again because they are not eating enough. The result is that a low metabolism tends to sink even lower, the body puts on more fat, and activity becomes more difficult – a classic vicious circle.

For those with high metabolic rates the reverse is true. With ad lib food and free-flowing energy, the liver deals with waste (and infections) quickly and efficiently. When adequate good food is available, the liver can increase its capacity and that of the rest of the metabolism, setting up a positive, beneficial cycle.

This is illustrated by the way the body deals with lactate. Fat-use in the muscle is limited by the build-up of lactate, a metabolic by-product which contributes to the sensation of muscular aches and tiredness. Trained muscles produce less lactate, but in addition, muscular wastes are moved away from working muscles to the liver more efficiently. And the benefits go further. The liver re-converts lactate to glycogen with increased efficiency, so that lactate becomes useful rather than a nuisance. Like all other such cycles, the lactate cycle benefits from regular use; which is one reason why the more exercise you do, the more enjoyable it becomes.

Smoking

Smoking affects the liver, as well as the heart and lungs. It causes one of the enzyme systems in the liver to speed up, allowing smokers to eat a little more without gaining weight. But the benefits are illusory because the imbalance produced in the liver means the body is deprived of nutrients and fat conservation is reinforced. Smoking doesn't stop you getting fat – but it does make it more difficult to grow thin again. Tobacco addiction results when slimmers use nicotine to calm edgy nerves.

Smoking is a bad idea. The main smoking and health messages are well known but there are specific points which are relevant to shedding fat. First, nicotine is a poison. The effects it produces in the liver are similar to those of DDT; in fact, nicotine can be used as an insecticide! Any poison will add to the load on the waste disposal capacity of your system. Any of the two hundred toxins in tobacco smoke could lead to the accumulation of persistent fat if your metabolism cannot cope.

Smoking reduces oxygen uptake from the lungs and then reduces the oxygen-carrying capacity of the blood. When you smoke, you inhale carbon monoxide, a poisonous gas. This combines with haemoglobin, the red pigment of the blood, to form carboxyhaemoglobin. Haemoglobin is the substance which carries oxygen round the body and when some of it is locked up by carbon monoxide, your oxygen-carrying capacity is greatly reduced. Smokers can reduce their blood oxygen level by up to 20%! The combination of reduced oxygen content with reduced blood flow caused by restricted

blood vessels puts smokers at a tremendous disadvantage when they try to get fit.

All the effects of smoking act against your best interests if you want to be slim. Active thin people do not
need a dangerous tranquilliser like nicotine: they keep
on an even keel through good nourishment and a well-
balanced life. If you're still smoking, give up now. Do
not worry about your weight: giving up tobacco is part
of the strategy that will make you slim for life.

By now you will realise that shedding fat is a matter of
total metabolic involvement. Indeed it is no exaggeration
to say that it involves every part of your being, all your
bodily systems and your mind in the way you perceive
yourself. In thinking and behaving like a thin person
you will change yourself, from the over-fat, low-energy,
hungry worrier about weight to the thin, active, high-
energy, confident person, too busy enjoying life to even
consider the irrelevant trivia, such as calories and scales,
which dominate the lives of fat failures.

How Your Hormones Benefit

Part of the change you will undergo will involve your
hormones. Hormones are chemical messengers which
control much of our bodily activity and behaviour. We
each have a personal hormone profile which contributes
to our unique individuality. The hormone profile of a fat
person is different from that of a thin person, so changing
from one to the other will mean re-balancing your
hormone profile to assist your new way of life.

With re-balanced hormones your transition from fat
to thin will be complete. Lest you should find this an
alarming prospect, let us reassure you. Hormones are
popularly thought of in terms of sex, and, while it is true
that they are deeply implicated in our sexuality, the sort
of changes we are talking about will have no adverse
effects on your sexual characteristics. Indeed the reverse
is more likely to be the case. One reward of a thin,

healthy body is a greatly enhanced capacity for sensual and sexual satisfaction. Like all of our functions this is improved by the correct, subtle balance being achieved by each individual. Overweight people have lost their balance. Some have lost it purposely, if not consciously, from fear or guilt about their sexuality. We will explore this further in Chapter Ten.

Hormones are intimately involved in fat metabolism. Fat is liberated from body stores by growth hormone. The importance of being active is that levels of growth hormone in the blood increase sharply about 10 to 15 minutes after you start vigorous activity. Growth hormone won't make you grow bigger (providing you have reached maturity) but it will promote the growth of lean tissue around your body, providing you are eating enough food! Under the influence of this hormone your body will shed fat and produce lithe, shapely muscles. And these muscles will have more mito-chondria, which means they will be able to burn yet more fat.

Once you become physically active other hormone changes occur, and all help you to remain a thin person. The effort of muscular exertion, ideally combined with the excitement of doing something you really enjoy, leads to the production of adrenalin and nor-adrenalin. These are the hormones that make you feel active and energetic (another example of the way the body produces positive reinforcement; becoming active makes you want to become active), they are popularly called the fight or flight hormones. You need neither fight nor flee, but you do need these hormones to facilitate shedding fat. Passion and worry also cause these hor-mones to be released, which is why lust, love or any other form of emotional stress can make you lose weight fast.

Insulin is another important hormone in fat metab-olism. Its production decreases with increased activty. This is important for shedding fat because insulin is the hormone which is primarily involved in fat storage. One of the objectives of the EAT YOURSELF THIN regime is that it reduces insulin production. This will both reduce your tendency to store fat, while at the same time encouraging your muscles to burn it. When blood insulin is high, your muscles will not burn fat, only glycogen; when insulin levels fall, fat can be released from stores for fuel.

One of the problems with a depressed metabolism is that high quantities of insulin are produced. This not only aids the accumulation of fat, but over long periods of time it can lead to mature onset diabetes. Eventually the body ceases to react to insulin and the over-fat person has to rely on artificial inputs; if they do not change and lose the fat (when they may also cease to be diabetic), they lay themselves open to a series of potentially fatal conditions. A depressed metabolism is not a healthy metabolism.

Let us try to survey the message of this chapter. You will have seen that being thin is a matter of your whole way of life. We cannot say it too often; if you want to be thin, think and behave like a thin person!

You will also have gathered that all of the systems involved in shedding fat and keeping it off benefit from use. It should also be clear that all these systems interact; a beneficial effect on one will help the others. You would be right to conclude that your body will react to improvement by further improvement.

At the heart of thin-person behaviour is eating enough food. You must do this to keep your metabolic fires alight, burning fat as efficiently as possible.

Your metabolism needs plenty of oxygen to work well (or inefficiently, in food terms). A healthy heart and lungs will deliver oxygen as required, provided you use them, and do not abuse them by smoking or neglect. Healthy blood vessels will deliver oxygen, nutrients and fat to your muscles so that they function at their best.

Body fat is burned in muscles. Add fuel from food, oxygen from blood, indulge in regular pleasurable activity, and you will burn fat. It is as simple as that.

All you need is the right ingredients, blended to suit your personal taste. We called you an artist because only you can get the final mix right for your personal needs. Our action plans later in the book will guide you on the right track, but the inspiration and success must be yours.

Living as a thin person will change you into a thin person. Your metabolism will lift to the level you require, and your hormone balance will adjust to suit your lifestyle. Things which once seemed impossible will gradually slide into perspective as enjoyable commonplaces, and you will gain the confidence to set yourself new goals on much wider horizons.

All this from eating more food? Of course! Food is life, the use of its energy produces everything that humanity has ever achieved. Correctly used, such a force can help achieve your desires. Isn't it great to know that the more you eat, the faster you can burn fat?

Summary

- Fat can only be used to produce energy; your muscles are the place where this energy is used.
- You need good muscle tone to burn fat and give good shape to your body.
- Muscles cannot burn fat alone – they need plenty of oxygen and glycogen. Glycogen comes from carbohydrate in food.
- Smoking damages vital capacity by cutting down on oxygen availability and reducing liver capacity. Smoking is *bad for your whole metabolism*.

Action Now

- *If you smoke – give up!*
- *Build up your oxygen levels by practising slow, deep breathing.*
- *Increase the length of time you spend walking.*

CHAPTER 6

Phase One – Eat Right

To EAT RIGHT, you must look carefully at your assumptions. You may have to revise your ideas about whether this or that food is good for you and whether it is fattening or not. Understanding food is fundamental to the change from fat- to thin-person thinking.

Most people do not eat the right food to stay slim. The right food must do two things: stop you feeling hungry and provide the nutrients you need. Because of wide individual variations in nutrient needs, we cannot set out a single simple diet that will guarantee success. What we can do is offer general guidance that will enable you to achieve your main objective, the loss of excess fat, without having to struggle for existence on a monotonous and unbalanced diet. You will be able to eat foods you like *and* improve your shape.

The first objective is to raise your metabolic rate. Whatever you are used to eating, your metabolic rate will increase when the nutritional value of your food improves. Take this small step and make sure you do not go hungry, and you will be on the road to success.

In this chapter we shall be concentrating on the *nutritional quality* of food. Start now by building more *fresh* food into your normal diet. Fresh fruit and nuts are nature's convenience foods, to eat whenever you feel peckish; they provide a wide range of vitamins, minerals and other nutrients to build up your general health and vitality.

If you are used to fast or convenience foods, changing to meals that include fresh vegetables will involve restructuring your lifestyle a little. If you have to eat out often and for convenience, seek out sources of more nutritious foods – for example opt for the salad bar rather than the burger in fast-food restaurants. You may have to break out of your regular pattern but the effort will be rewarded by its effects on your metabolism.

We shall explain what we believe to be the *ideal* way for you to eat. However, we do recognise that the ideal will not always be available. What is important is that if you cannot get the ideal, you should always aim for the best you can get. *Improve* the quality of your food and remember that a relative improvement will produce worthwhile benefits. Your food should meet your nutritional needs without loading you with fattening junk, so that it underwrites your health in the widest sense. The typical modern diet fails to meet these requirements. Eating has become a minefield of hazardous choices; every few months some new warning appears about problems with yet another component of the modern diet, from fat to additives. The past decades represent a trail of anxiety for those who are concerned about the adverse effects of modern food on health. But this continuing criticism has produced a growing reaction against trends in food production and you can now get good food if you look for it.

Choose Wholefoods

Fresh fruit, vegetables and nuts are wholefoods: you can eat them complete or with very little preparation. But most of our staple foods have been processed by the food industry before we buy them. This processing can remove their nutritional value, creating fattening foods from nourishing ingredients.

Wholefoods tend to be brown whereas the processed equivalents are white. This is because the brown parts which contain the vitamins, minerals and fibre are removed and sold in other products – even as food supplements. Removing the most essential ingredients from basic foodstuffs clearly makes no nutritional sense, but it does make financial sense to the food industry.

Wholefoods are left as naturally complete as possible.

They have been processed least, or had nothing extracted from the basic ingredients during preparation. They therefore contain more nutrients than their processed counterparts: more vitamins, more minerals and more fibre. As a consequence, they are more satisfying, more nutritious and less fattening. Wholemeal bread, for example, is undoubtedly better for you than chalky white. It contains the germ and the bran from the original grains from which it was made, whereas white bread contains starch and little else. The carbohydrate in white flour products is fattening because the nutrients you need to turn it into energy are processed out of them. In contrast, when you eat bread made from wholemeal flour, you get the vitamins and minerals you need for energy, with carbohydrate in the best form for the body to use.

The Ideal Food is Organic Food

Fortunately, not all the food industry sees the balance sheet as its primary product. A sizeable and rapidly growing part of the farming and food supply industry is based on the proposition that good food is inseperable from good health. These people supply *organic foods*.

Organic wholefoods are the very best. No chemicals are used in their production; they will not smuggle toxins into your body and they are rich in minerals. Go for them whenever you can.

Why We Believe Organic Food is Best

Organically produced food *naturally* contains all the nutrients we need to be well fed. Organically grown vegetables may not appear as plastic-perfect as their chemical-drenched counterparts, but they taste better and are better for you. Organically produced meat has additional advantages. It is free from drug residues and the animals are raised without the cruelty of conventional factory farming. As far as possible, organic livestock live the sort of life nature intended; because organic farmers do not use drugs, they cannot subject their animals to conditions that would make them sick.

Organic food will not smuggle toxins and pollutants into your body, nor will it leave you with hidden hungers. This is the ideal we should all aim for. But because the conventional food industry is not organic, you may have to make a special effort to find supplies. Fortunately, more and more shops are selling organic food and some supermarkets have organic food counters. If you have difficulty finding sources of produce, consult *The New Organic Food Guide* by Alan Gear (Dent) or *The Green Consumer Guide* by John Elkington and Julia Hailes (Gollancz).

We do not live in an ideal world and you are unlikely to be able to change to a totally organic diet. Try to change as many items of your basic food as you can and keep pressing shopkeepers for more; shops are changing and more pressure will help.

Taste and Nutrient Deficiency

Wholefoods taste different from processed foods. Processed foods contain flavourings and flavour-enhancing chemicals that disguise the essential blandness or unpleasantness of their denatured ingredients. But the taste of food also depends on your ability to detect subtleties of flavour, which in turn depends on the quality of your diet. Changing to better quality food may mean changing your beliefs about how food *should* taste.

Friends who stay with us are fed mainly organic food, with never an additive in sight. At first their main reaction is to the quantity we eat and its freshness, not its taste. But if they stay a week or two their reaction changes; they begin to comment on the range of flavours they are experiencing. They begin to enjoy food more. When they return to their normal lives, many comment on the nastiness of food they had previously eaten.

If our friends live on a typical modern diet, as regrettably many do, one effect is that is damages their sense of taste. Zinc deficiency is particularly to blame for this and it is believed to be very common. So the modern adulterated diet not only robs people of many nutrients, but in doing so it inhibits their ability to taste just how bad most processed foods are. If they also suffer allergies or immune system problems because of the chemical overload, their sense of taste will be further damaged if the sense of smell fades away as well. For smokers, the problem of discriminating good food from junk becomes practically impossible. Food producers win both ways with the modern diet: they create consumers who are incapable of discriminating between nutritious and impoverished food, and who cannot detect the foul flavours of chemicals and residues.

You will discover that after a few weeks on organic wholefoods your sense of taste returns. You will wonder how people can eat those 'flavour-enhanced' prep-arations that are a perversion of real food – particularly when real food is positively good for you.

Let us summarise: the ideal type of food you should go for is food which is organically produced. As far as possible you should eat wholefoods. And as much of your food as possible should be fresh. A diet with the major proportion of its content made up of these foods will provide the nutrients you require.

There are wide variations in needs for specific nutri-ents; sometimes one person may need ten times the quantity of a particular nutrient as another. Some food and diet industry experts believe you can live on junk foods and make up for the deficiencies by popping vitamin pills or diet supplements. The problem with this approach is that, although you may know what the food lacks, you are unlikely to know what your body needs. While we acknowledge that nutritional sup-plements may be necessary for some people under certain circumstances, they are no substitute for good food. The only solution is to eat the best possible food and to learn to trust your appetite. It will usually give you the right cues for the sorts of foods which you should be eating. But enough highly nutritious food will provide a good basis for a slim and healthy life.

Basic Nutrition

What does your body expect from its food? The substances we need can be roughly divided into two groups, the *macronutrients* and the *micronutrients*. Both are important and your final objective must be to find the right balance for you and the way you live.

Macronutrients are the substances we consume in relatively large quantities: carbohydrates, proteins and fats. When these are properly in balance in the diet, the micronutrients tend to be provided automatically. In unadulterated foods all the nutrients come in the same package. If you think about it, this makes natural sense. Our primitive ancestors did not go around with nutrient lists (or calorie counters), they relied on their senses and appetites to guide them, and the foods they selected did the rest. You have to regain that natural trust in your senses. This is why organic foods are so good: they deliver what your senses expect, and your senses will tell you what your body needs.

In each of the macro food groups there are types of that particular food which are good and others which are bad. You must aim for the *best* and settle for the good when the best is unattainable. You should think very hard before including anything else in your diet. You are what you eat; only the best should be good enough.

Carbohydrate is the crucial fuel. It is essential to light up your metabolic furnace and keep it burning brightly. It is the easiest fuel for the body to use; it can provide energy for every tissue, and while some parts of the body can derive energy from other sorts of fuel, the brain can only use carbohydrate. Carbohydrate is essential to fire up the muscles and keep them running so that they can burn fat.

If you are a seasoned dieter you will have read a lot about carbohydrate; you may have learned to regard it as bad and fattening. Many diets restrict carbohydrate severely in order to induce rapid weight (mainly water) loss. Unfortunately carbohydrate restriction will not lead to rapid *fat* loss, because as we explained in the previous chapter, you need carbohydrate to burn fat.

Carbohydrates come in two basic forms: they are either simple or complex. It is important to be able to tell the difference between them. While all carbohydrates are made up of carbon, hydrogen and oxygen, roughly in similar proportions, the molecules formed by these chemicals come in many different shapes and sizes. The simplest carbohydrates are the sugars. These have very small molecules which can pass through membranes in the body very easily.

The ease of absorption causes much of the problem with sugars. When you eat (or drink) sugar, it is absorbed through the membranes of your mouth. Suck a sweet, and those molecules slide straight into your blood stream through the walls of tiny blood vessels. Sugars do not need any further processing to get straight into your brain. We have no defences, no discrimination; they are an instant hit. This is why they can be very addictive and very disturbing to your whole metabolism.

Think about sugars from your body's point of view. In nature pure sugars are very rare. Usually sugars would be found in fruits and in eating them we help the plant disperse its seeds. But there would be a relatively small amount of sugar in a natural diet. The body has many interlinked systems designed specifically to maintain an optimum blood sugar level. Too much sugar is damaging: those little molecules can upset the whole biological balance of cells. So your body gets rid of excess sugar by secreting insulin from the pancreas. Insulin scavenges sugar from the blood and puts it into specialised cells where it can be made safe and stored for possible future use. You know those spongy specialised storage cells; they store sugar as fat.

People with extremely high metabolic rates, like super-energetic teenagers or athletes, can cope with simple sugars, although it would be better if they found other sources of energy. The rest of us have to avoid them; simple sugars short-circuit the best run metabolisms and the results can be disasterous.

Although we say you should eat more, *refined simple sugars are prohibited*. Eating right means banishing from your life sweets, sweet drinks (including 'diet' versions and artificial sweeteners), cakes and biscuits, and everything else made with sugar. Ordinary sugar has the chemical name **sucrose**; avoid it. Also avoid **glucose**; despite its 'healthy' image, it is as unhealthy as sucrose. If you were to do this and nothing else, there is a very good chance your fat would melt away. And you would reduce your risk of heart disease, diabetes and tooth decay. If you need further convincing try reading, *Pure, White and Deadly* by John Yudkin (Davis-Poynter).

Not, we hasten to add, that you are expected to live without sweet things. Certainly not! It is the source of the sweetness that you must choose carefully. As we mentioned earlier, fruit is the traditional source of dietary sugar, and this is a good source of unrefined carbohydrate to fuel your body. You must eat whole fruits though, because the fruit sugar, **fructose**, is packaged in fruit with many other nutrients that enhance health and fuel your metabolism.

Different fruits offer different benefits. Many contain vitamins C and A, potassium, which is essential for the proper biochemical balance of the body (bananas are a particularly good source), and trace minerals such as boron which is essential for bone strength. Citrus fruit contains bioflavinoids which enhance healing and immunity. Apples, pears and plums contain pectins which protect us from pollutants such as lead and keep our intestines working well. The list goes on: each different type of fruit confers benefits. The principle is that fruit is good for you; it should be your only source of simple sugars.

You should be aware that eating large quantities of fruit can cause problems. If you munch through a pound of sweet fruit at a sitting, you are likely to absorb enough fructose to set off an insulin reaction that could send it into store. Fruit sugar is bound together with fibre which slows its absorption and keeps blood sugar fairly even, but it can make you fat if you have too much. Try to aim for about a pound of fruit a day, but spread it throughout the day as snacks. If it is not organically grown you should peel it. Although the peel is especially nutritious, it will have been sprayed with all sorts of horrors which could add to fat and cause other problems. Regrettably, even thorough washing is unlikely to remove the residues of pesticide sprays.

Complex carbohydrates are made of long-chain molecules which have to be broken down by digestion before they can be absorbed. Because of this they enter the body more slowly than simple sugars and the body responds differently to them. Despite this crucial difference many dieticians lump all the carbohydrates together. This does not make sense to us, nor does it make sense to your body.

EATING YOURSELF THIN depends upon a high carbohydrate diet. But this means a diet high in complex carbohydrates, the foods that do make sense to your body.

Let us explain why. Complex carbohydrates are mainly found in wholefoods derived from plants which contain large amounts of fibre. This fibre cannot be digested in the stomach or top parts of the intestine. This slows down the absorption of complex carbohydrates to a rate which your body can comfortably handle. This means there is no danger of an insulin surge; even large amounts of complex carbohydrates will only induce a gradual release of insulin, followed by a gradual fall. Your blood sugar will remain constant and there will be no dumping into fat.

Complex carbohydrates are the best source of energy because they maintain muscle glycogen, those local fuel stores essential for pleasureable activity. And because they provide a slow release of sugar to the blood, they are also ideal fuel for the brain which cannot cope with massive surges alternating with deprivation. Complex carbohydrates will also improve your general demeanour. If you suffer from problems associated with *low* blood sugar, such as dizziness, irritability, poor concentration, and even blackouts, you may avoid them completely by eating complex carbohydrates in snacks throughout the day. Because of their physiological make-up, most women would be better off eating little but often, rather than going without for hours, then eating large meals which occupy their digestion for hours.

Best of all for anyone with fat to lose are the slowest-acting complex carbohydrates. These are found in foods with the highest fibre content such as beans, oats and starchy vegetables. The best high-fibre foods are not obviously fibrous, like celery and bran; the most valuable forms of nutritional fibre are actually sticky, jelly-like substances. Oatmeal is very high in top quality natural fibre, as is porridge (unsweetened of course) – try it in the traditional way with added wheatgerm and salt if you find it otherwise too bland – and also oatflake-based dishes like muesli will keep your blood sugar on a wonderfully even keel.

The high-energy, high-fibre foods which are important to your diet include all types of unrefined wholegrain products; peas, beans and lentils of all types; all vegetables including potatoes (if you buy organic you can eat the nutritious skins as well); brown rice and rice cakes; and of course, fruit.

These sorts of food should predominate because they provide energy and they will raise your metabolic rate safely. Eat them whenever you feel hungry, in whatever quantities you wish – though you may have to go easy on the fruit if, like us, you adore it!

Let us summarise once more: you should aim to eat organically produced foods, especially wholefoods, and you must get enough complex carbohydrates, the slower acting the better. Eat little but often until a pattern emerges which suits your lifestyle and needs.

You also need **proteins**. These have been described as 'the building blocks of life' because every living thing is made up of them. Proteins are long complex molecules with a great variety of constituents. All contain carbon, hydrogen and oxygen, as do carbohydrates, but proteins also have nitrogen and other elements such as sulphur and phosphorus. So in addition to building and maintaining your body, proteins provide many valuable elements and micronutrients.

Few people in Western countries get too little protein because all our staple foods contain some of it. If you had a very unusual and unbalanced diet of only fruit and vegetables, without nuts, grains, seeds, fish or meat, you would go short of protein. But you would be short of total energy input too. Protein malnutrition usually develops in combination with general malnutrition due to starvation.

If you are a strict vegetarian or a vegan, you should be careful to chose suitable combinations of plant proteins. In general you should eat plenty of pulses (peas, beans, lentils) with grains such as rice and wholewheat, and make sure you get enough seeds and nuts. Seeds and nuts are particularly rich sources of protein.

The problem with traditional sources of protein – meat, poultry, dairy produce, and farmed trout and salmon – is that (unless organically produced) it will contain drug and chemical residues. All conventional meat is produced with drugs and hormones; the fodder the animals are fed is polluted with chemical residues and these build up in the meat and milk to be passed on to you. If you eat these products and cannot find organic sources, eat as little as possible. Go for the leanest meat and remove more fat by cutting, cooking and skimming; avoid liver and kidneys, as these organs concentrate pollutants. Poultry is better if it is free-range and fish is usually the best option; fish fats are valuable for health despite the pollution in the seas around our islands. Go for skimmed milk; cows also store pollutants in fat and express them in the fat in milk. Cheese consumption should be kept low. Go for small quantities of good quality, high flavour cheese, preferably low-fat varieties such as mature Gouda rather than bland mass-produced types which are high in fat.

How much protein do you need to live as a thin person? There is much debate on this question and no simple answer, because people vary so much. The body can use proteins for energy rather than building. It does this by splitting up the molecules to remove the nitrogen atoms, thus turning proteins into carbohydrates. In some people, the metabolism frequently opts for this pathway; they thrive on a high protein diet. Others prefer their carbohydrate in a more basic form and do not feel at their best with too much protein. Usually men can cope with more protein than women. Once more it is a question of finding your individual balance, and this depends on how you feel. Listen to the messages from your body and follow your appetite. Go for the balance that gives you the most lasting energy.

It is essential to get enough protein when you are burning fat. The sulphur-containing proteins are particularly important but they are damaged by heat; good sources are eggs, nuts and seeds. Raw nuts are best; a handful a day is a good idea. Boiled free-range eggs are also valuable; ideally, you should cook them until the white is set (otherwise it can strip your system of vitamins) and the yolk, source of the sulphur-containing proteins, is soft. These proteins are needed to make **glutathione**, a substance that enables your liver to cope with hazardous wastes which may be produced by fat metabolism. Your need for glutathione increases when you are burning fat, but most slimming diets actually cause the level in the liver to fall precipitously because they do not provide the nutrients necessary to maintain it.

Fats are the third macro component of our food. In recent years much attention has been paid to fats; saturated versus unsaturated, animal versus vegetable, and so on. Fats have become a highly controversial area, where vested interests and their many claims go far beyond scientific evidence.

The controversy over fat is stimulated by the fact that many diseases, including cancers and heart disease, are linked with a high-fat diet. There is direct conflict of interests between health and the food industry lobby. The fat content of the modern diet has increased to around 40% over the past few decades. This is one of the reasons why there are so many fat people today, and why the demands for treatment always outrun resources for care.

Yet despite the general down on fat, it is very important physiologically. Quite simply, our bodies would not work without it. Fat is the crucial component in every cell membrane and the foundation of all our nervous tissues; our brains are mainly cholesterol.

Problems arise with dietary fats when the body tries to use the wrong sorts of fats or when the fats are polluted or chemically changed. Make no mistake about it, fat can make you fat just as quickly as sugar, although the metabolic mechanism is different. The modern diet, with its combination of hidden fats and simple refined carbohydrate, is a disasterously fattening mixture; living on biscuits, cakes, fast foods, puddings and chocolate, with ad lib sweetened coffee or colas (including 'diet' versions) is a certain recipe for piling on pounds of fat.

But a diet too low in the right types of fat will also damage your health and lower your energy levels. Certain types of fat are essential for metabolism and your body cannot create them. These are the **essential fatty acids**.

Essential fatty acids are found in oily fish, such as herring and mackerel; in oily vegetables like avocadoes and olives; in nuts, seeds and wheatgerm. Going short on essential fatty acids will damage your body's repair systems. When you become more active on your high-energy diet you will need good repair and rebuilding systems to improve the quality of your lean flesh, so start building up your reserves now!

Foods high in essential fatty acids will give you the bonus of a range of fat-soluble nutrients and minerals which are often short in the British diet. Nuts, in particular, are some of the richest sources of trace minerals available. It is strange that nuts are regarded as mere snack foods; in our opinion they should be among the basic staples of our diet.

Convenient sources of essential fatty acids are the minimally processed vegetable oils. Cold-pressed organic olive or sunflower oil can be used for just about all cooking and salad dressings. Although vegetable oils are generally less contaminated than animal fats, they also may be chemically modified. Fats can be changed into more hazardous forms by cooking and processing. The worst is fat which is continually reheated; this produces oxidised fats that can disrupt normal cell development. Everyone who values their health should avoid foods like chips, which are impregnated with oxidised fats. They are associated with heart disease and cancers.

Minerals, vitamins, and other micronutrients form a wide group of essential dietary substances. While we do not need to know how much of each we should consume, high-energy living does demand that we get the full range. Too much is better than too little; the body can always shed excess, but it cannot make up for deficiencies.

In general, our broad recommendations on carbohydrates, proteins and fats will ensure that you automatically get enough micronutrients. However, as you are changing your lifestyle to that of a thin person, you should be aware of those which are relevant to you.

You should ensure you get enough **zinc, iron** and **selenium**. Vegetarians may run short of them. Dark green leafy vegetables are good sources of iron, and watercress is high in many minerals. Vegetarians will get much of their zinc from nuts, seeds and organically grown wholegrains. Wholegrains and fish are good sources of selenium.

Vitamins which are important to the EAT YOURSELF THIN strategy are those involved with energy production, tissue building, de-toxification and waste disposal. The mitochondrial enzyme systems which produce energy depend on B-group vitamins. There is no single source of B vitamins; some are found in wholegrains and wheat- or oat-germ, others in leafy vegetables, and yeast contains a potent brew. Supplement your diet with wheatgerm and brewers' yeast (from your local health shop) if you feel your body needs help converting carbohydrate to energy. Vitamins A, C and E and folic acid (a B-group vitamin) are necessary for tissue building and detoxification. You will get these from fruit, fresh vegetables, and nuts, so make sure you eat some of these foods every day.

What you drink is as important as what you eat. There is much individual variability in response to some common drinks. Our general advice is to cut to the absolute minimum your intake of tea and coffee, and substitute herb teas, mineral water or pure fruit juices. Fruit juices are best extended by diluting 50/50 with mineral water, such as Perrier. Tea or soft drinks with meals interfere with mineral absorption, whereas orange or grapefruit juice will increase your uptake of zinc from food.

If you cannot give up tea or coffee completely the best strategy is to go for quality. Choose real coffee and experiment with exotic teas. When you have found brands you like, have them in small quantities as an anticipated experience. Get away from pouring brown sludgy liquids down you as an unthinking habit.

Coffee may be particularly troublesome for over-fat people. It reduces micronutrient uptake and can have a potent fat-creating effect on those sensitive to it. We have known people who lost pads of fat as if by magic after giving up coffee. Coffee can be difficult to give up:

withdrawal symptoms for regular drinkers often include a severe headache for a day or so. If you suspect coffee is a villain in your fat problem, you may be amazed and delighted by the results in weeks subsequent to giving it up. Abdominal discomfort and bloating can be due to after-dinner coffee, while sleeping problems and agitation are common. De-caffeinated coffee may not be the answer; caffeine is just one of a range of metabolically active chemicals in coffee.

On the other hand, if you are not sensitive to it, coffee can actually help burn fat. A cup half an hour before activity will mobilise fat faster. However, if you are sensitive the problems caused will outweigh this potential benefit. Coffee is a drug that should only be used in small amounts, and it is not good for everyone. You are the only person who can judge whether it is good or bad for you.

While shedding fat you should keep your intake of alcohol to an absolute minimum. Alcohol has to be metabolised by the liver and this is a difficult task if your liver is also rearranging itself to metabolise fat and deal with the waste from that. The last thing it needs on top is a couple of stiff drinks. Toxic stress and dumping into fat could be the result. Occasional drinking can have social benefits that raise your general vitality. In our culture most people believe they do a little better if they drink a little, and mortality statistics show that occasional drinkers live longer than teetotalers. But you must be careful with alcohol; it is a potent drug, as well as potentially fattening. Dilute with fruit juice or mineral water (not 'diet' or low-calorie mixers); have long drinks and make them last.

Finally, two considerations which should not be overlooked. First, cooking. Cooking, in the traditional sense of bringing many ingredients together to create a meal of several courses, is fading from many peoples' everyday lives. Either they lack the time, and the convenience offered by packaged food – the consumer's small reward for the industry's far greater convenience – have left the kitchen as a gleaming but under-used status symbol. You can use this modern trend to your advantage, because from a nutritional viewpoint, the less cooking the better! Cooking tends to remove nutrients, so wherever possible fruits and vegetables should be eaten raw. When you do need to cook, face up to it, and do it well, using only the best ingredients – remember, the things you are preparing are going to be part of you.

The second consideration is freshness. It is regrettably true that the best food is food which will go bad. You must buy fresh supplies of fruit and vegetables regularly. Always go for new supplies; new-dug potatoes, for example, contain four times as much vitamin C as those from store. Additionally, stored vegetables, unless they are organic, will have been sprayed with anti-fungal toxins and chemicals to preserve them or prevent further growth. These should be avoided. Only *naturally* fresh food has the special benefits of high vitamin content.

Taking on board all this information about food may take time and effort. This is part of the price of changing from a fat person to a thin one; this knowledge is essential. It will help you to stay slim and healthy for the rest of your life.

A last thought on food. Have you thought of growing your own? No matter where you live it is possible to do something. Growing your own ensures both freshness and quality. In addition, gardening, as millions know, can be an enjoyable open-air activity – and there are few fat gardeners! So if you have access to a plot of ground that is not close to industrial or major road pollution, get your own organic production unit going. Even a few square feet of ground will provide salads and strawberries. If you have no land, you can still grow some crops on window sills and in the airing cupboard; we get crunchy nourishing beansprouts in three days from mung and azuki beans sprouted in an old coffee jar. Your ingenuity could work wonders in this direction.

Having selected the right types of food, rearranged your shopping list and changed the culinary habits of a fat person for those of the new thin you, when should you eat your new nutritious food, and how much should you eat at a time? The next chapter will tell you.

Summary

- Understanding about food is essential to your change from fat- to slim-person eating.
- The ideal foods are organically produced wholefoods. Go for these whenever possible. If not available, go for freshness and quality.
- Eat plenty of complex carbohydrates – wholefoods from plant sources; avoid simple sugars.
- Make sure you have a good supply of essential fatty acids from fish, nuts, cold-pressed vegetable oils; avoid animal fats and chemically treated fats whenever possible.

Action Now

- *Gradually increase the proportion of complex carbohydrate in your diet by eating larger portions of vegetables and wholegrain cereals.*
- *Make sure you are getting enough protein, vitamins and minerals to balance your intake of complex carbohydrates: fish and free-range eggs are good sources.*

CHAPTER 7

Phase Two – Eat More!

EATING MORE IS at the heart of the EAT YOURSELF THIN strategy. Now is the time to harden your resolve and reject any lingering fat-person attitudes and reactions. You will recall that dieting does not make you thin, it gives you more fat; that hunger prepares your body for famine and depresses your metabolic rate; that a low metabolic rate conserves fat, deprives you of energy and turns life into a lack-lustre experience. Eating more will do the opposite of all these undesirable things.

Eating more of the right foods, at the right time, in the right quantities, will generate the right metabolic profile for the lifestyle you want. It is the only way to live the life of a thin person. The right foods were explained in the previous chapter, the right time and quantities will depend upon your personal needs, and the metabolic profile produced will depend upon the complete lifestyle you adopt.

Let us deal with the question of when you should eat. First, you should not put off eating until late in the day. This is typical fat-person behaviour; fat people believe that delaying, with its inevitable hunger, will help limit their food intake. Whether it does or does not is irrelevant; the probable result is that you will eat too much at one time when you do finally allow yourself to have a meal, and you may fall for poor-quality sweet or fatty food as you try to satisfy your hunger. This will produce an insulin surge which will cause the body to store more of your food as fat.

You should get up in time to have a good – that means enjoyable – breakfast; this will give you energy to get your day going. And have a nourishing lunch. Don't starve yourself at tea time either. When dinner or supper time comes round you won't be ravenous; you will be able to choose foods that your body wants to meet your nutrient needs rather than falling for the desperate rush of sweet or fatty foods.

Second, you should eat frequently. This is particularly relevant for women. Far back in our evolutionary past the patterns of eating for men and women took slightly different paths. Male and female bodies fuel themselves differently, men relying on large muscles and liver with a lot of glycogen, women relying on subcutaneous fat *combined with current-account energy from food.*

Because of these differences, women should tend to be vegetarian nibblers, rather than meat-eating feasters. The three-meals-a-day regime is typically male, and not very good for females.

You must keep enough food energy in circulation to meet your needs. This is why eating enough is so crucial if you wish to remain thin. Too little, and your body will lower its metabolic rate and conserve energy as fat; too much, and it will raise the metabolic rate and offer you more energy. To burn fat you must go with this energy rise and use it to maintain a higher metabolic rate. But you must also be careful, because excesses which outrun your metabolic rate could get stored as fat.

So you should eat frequent small meals, relying on your body messages to tell you how much to eat. The aim should be to adjust food intake to keep just ahead of need, so that you always have some positive reserve in the system. If you feel hungry, the message is clear: you are not eating enough.

Snacking at frequent intervals can cause problems. Unless you gear your food preparation to this you could fall back on convenience snacks, some of the worst sorts of fast junk food. Nibble on fresh raw fruits and vegetables; this is where seeds and nuts come into their own. You can also build snacks around rice cakes and sandwiches made with wholemeal bread. Or have low-fat natural yoghurt with fruit or wheatgerm or grain flakes – or all three.

Massive meals should always be avoided. Not only do they swamp that delicate feedback mechanism, giving you confused messages, but starving then gorging produces the sort of blood-sugar variations which maximise fat deposition. Many cultures where food is important, such as the French, understand this; if they are going to have a celebratory feast they spend most of the day at it, so that if they eat (and drink) a lot it is spread out and mixed with talk and dancing. This is a much better approach than two or three large platefuls while the news is on TV. Instead of large meals and hungry gaps, you should aim for a gentle tickover, where you are neither hungry nor stuffed. When you have achieved this with frequent portions of good food, fruit and fresh vegetables, you will be pushing your metabolic processes up to higher energy levels.

What is the right quantity to eat? You may already be eating the right quantities, but of the wrong sorts of food. If this is so, eating right may have solved many of your problems. But for the majority, accustomed to an ethos of food restriction, there can only be one general answer: you need to eat more than you are eating now. How much more will depend on a variety of factors, such as how much fat you are carrying, how old you are, your general body type, and how active you are capable of becoming. It will also depend upon what effects changing the sorts of food you eat has had on your metabolism and shape.

Let us give some broad outlines. If you are in your twenties, with no children, and have been an occasional dieter, then you should aim to increase your food intake by perhaps 50% (up to around 2,000 calories) over a period of four weeks. You should use your increased energy for more physical activity, when your food intake should go up higher. Your fat problem is very easy to resolve – you may do it just by eating right and using the energy this produces.

If you are at the other extreme, beyond forty, have had several children, been up and down on the diet seesaw for years, hate physical activity and lack raw vitality, you must aim for gradual change. Your main problem is likely to be the ingrained habits and assumptions built up over years, and the subjection of your needs to those of your family. For you the change to good *quality* food must be the first aim; this may take some weeks. Once you are eating right and you have changed your eating timing to that outlined above, then you should increase your intake above its current level by between 15 and 25% per month until you are up to 50%. You will have a more gradual increase in activity, starting with basic breathing (Appendix B) and going on to more ambitious burning as your metabolism picks up.

Bear in mind that how much you actually eat is not important, as long as you eat a little more than enough. Those enzymes in the mitochondria of your cells have to be primed before they will get to work, and their priming comes from the direct input of what you eat. What the quantity is will vary from day to day as your energy demands change and circumstances around you alter. We all need more food in cold weather; we all need more when working under stress or when playing hard. Conversely we need less when relaxing in the sun or preoccupied with emotional turmoil.

To fix the final amount that is right for you, you have to get to know yourself. This is the true occupation of the artist of the self; you must understand what it is you are working with in the self-creation of your ideal.

As your confidence with food grows, you will hear the messages of your body more clearly, and as your body changes and becomes closer to your ideal you will respond without the need to think. Just as you respond automatically to many other things in life, so you will to your personal food needs. But you must give yourself time; remember what you are doing is creating a new self with a new way of life, that of a healthy, lean, active person. The way of the dyed-in-the-wool fat person is to look for the quick, easy answer. There are no such answers; that is why they remain fat no matter what they try. You are working on the final answer to fat, it will take time, but the results will be permanent.

There are some body messages you should beware of, those false messages of addiction. These can be stimulated by foods and substances in foods which can have exactly the same effects as drugs. We mentioned the effect of coffee in the last chapter, but sugar, salt, chocolate and some food additives can also produce addictive reactions in many people. The addictive reaction is like a roller-coaster; when your system is down, it nags to go up again, only to crash down after the particular hit the substance causes. Parts of your metabolism can enjoy this and will give you a hard time if you do not give in. The only answer, if the addiction is contributing to your fat, is to break free. Use a holiday, or other change in wider circumstances, to knock the substance out of your life. The best answer to addictive nagging is to eat some fruit and nuts; the carbohydrates and micronutrients will fill the metabolic pathways. Dieters do not do this because they think such things are fattening; they remain trapped with their fat and their addiction.

The objective of eating more of the right foods is to create a new metabolic profile. Changing your eating habits and eating right will have initiated this process; eating more will complete it. From being depressed, your metabolism will swing back and start to lift. As those enzymes become primed, and the mitochrondia produce energy, you will *feel* better. Your whole body will start to function better as well; you will sleep better at night when all the nutrients your body needs for repair and recuperation are readily available. You will wake in the morning with more energy, so you will be able to use your day more effectively. This will leave you more time for yourself. These are the benefits that flow from a positive cycle; the exact opposite of the tremendous amount of time which can be lost through the inefficiency that comes from poor mental and physical functioning caused by poor nutrition.

The benefits of this dietary change have been demonstrated by nutritionists at the Brighton Premenstrual Tension Advisory Service. They treat women with severe PMT (who are often over-fat) with a diet very similar to the one we recommend. To their surprise – but not ours – they discovered that these women began to shed excess fat. Sometimes they had difficulty persuading women to eat the high-calorie foods recommended; many would baulk at eating nuts, bananas and wholegrains. They feared that they would put on even more fat. In fact, eating these nutrient-rich foods and increasing the total energy content of the diet produced weight loss as well as curing pre-menstrual problems, especially among the most obese women.

When you get your metabolic rate rising, you will find that you move faster and achieve more with less effort. Life will become less of a struggle and you will find yourself meeting challenges that defeated you before. The energising effects of good food affects your mind and body simultaneously. When you are mentally alert, your brain's hormone balance changes so that you burn food faster and get more physical energy from it. Eating enough top quality wholefoods, which naturally contain all the nutrients necessary for maximum energy availability, ensures that you get the fuel that will turn the spark of your rising metabolism into a fire.

Oxygen

However, fire does not burn with fuel alone. Without oxygen there can be no flame, but the more oxygen there is the hotter the flame will burn. To use your rising metabolic furnace to burn fat, you have to give it as much oxygen as it can use.

In addition to not eating enough food, many people do not get enough oxygen into their bodies to maximise their energy availability. The most common problem is shallow breathing, where the lungs are rarely properly filled. Many factors in modern life conspire to discourage deep breathing: sitting in office chairs, in the car, or in front of TV.

Sitting for long periods interferes with oxygen availability; you will keep your mental and physical energy at a higher level if you have breaks at intervals. If you work in an office, pace your work so that every hour or so you can go for a walk around and do a breathing routine. Don't worry about wasting time; it will soon be apparent that your performance is going up, even if you appear to be doing less. You could suggest that others try the same routine; it works for everybody. When writing we get caught at our desks for long periods, but we find that if we get up, stretch and stroll and breathe deep for a few minutes every hour or so, we can keep going longer.

What will be the most noticeable effect of increasing the oxygen input to your body? You have probably guessed – you will feel hungry. When this happens it is a good sign; it means you are using the energy from your food, the oxygen is pushing up your metabolic rate and demanding more fuel to give you more energy. Keep the positive cycle going, have a tasty snack and enjoy the good feelings that awaken in your body.

Smoking, as we have already explained, is the worst thing you can do to your oxygen levels. While fewer men are smoking cigarettes, it is tragic that more young women are getting hooked. If you still smoke, remind yourself that you are damaging your body's capacity to produce energy; smokers may get a little, but they lose a lot. Do not be afraid to give up. In the not-so-long term you will look and feel better; your energy levels will be higher than those you leave coughing and wheezing behind, and you will be able to burn fat faster.

If you decide to stop smoking at the same time as starting to EAT YOURSELF THIN, you will be able to minimise the misery of nicotine withdrawal. There is no denying that nicotine is a powerful drug, and coming off it can hurt. Starting so many other new things will help you to give up.

Your goal must be total abstinence from tobacco. There are no effective half measures. If you just cut down, you are fooling yourself but not your body; you are still a smoker. The number of smokes will climb back to what it was before you tried to put the brakes on. Time and again we have seen acquaintances who smoke waste effort on cutting down without making the final and irrevocable decision to quit; all have reverted. Those who have succeeded in giving up (including ourselves) told themselves on a particular day that they would not have another cigarette. Full stop.

Active Enjoyment

As your energy levels rise and your body begins to feel more alive, you will reach a point where you will have to look for ways of being more active. If you are a hard-pressed mother, or working full-time, you may not see how more is possible. This is because you are still in conflict with your body, you are holding it back, and it is doing the same to you. When you are eating right, eating more, and getting your metabolic fires burning with more oxygen, you will begin to feel growing urges to *do* things, just as the young bird must use its wings, although it has never flown before.

When you reach this stage you should congratulate yourself; you are well on the way to being a thin person. Why not celebrate? How about thinking about something you have always had a secret desire to do, skiing or horse riding, walking those beautiful places only accessible on foot, or (as they used to say) cutting a real dash on the dance floor? Now your dream of being a thin person is changing to reality it is time to dream the next dream and to start making it come true. Use the energy that is pushing for an outlet in ways which help burn more of that fat, and at the same time prepare to do whatever your desire leads you towards; find out where you can do it, what you need to know, sort out training or classes. In short, get yourself equipped to enjoy being thin and active.

You may still have doubts about being a physically active person. In our sluggish, unhealthy and over-fat world this is regrettably common. We are amazed when we go skating occasionally that we are among the few adults on the rink; most seem to sit like premature geriatrics watching children having all the fun. We are not against children having fun, but we insist on having our share as well, and so should you! Do not worry about being shown up, children are very tolerant of adult learners; indeed they are usually most helpful. And if you go skiing you cannot avoid the local four-year-olds showing you how it should be done. Forget foolish and inhibiting pride; think about fun and adventure instead, and enjoy *yourself*.

The physical activity in the EAT YOURSELF THIN strategy is based upon the pleasure principle. Enjoyable activity encourages you to become more active; the more active you are the more fat you will shed, and the more active you will become. We hope you will become as hooked on the pleasures of using your body as we are. Eventually you will reach a stable plateau, where food, activity, in fact your whole lifestyle, are in a balance which is right for you.

To get to this point pleasurably you need all the ingredients we have covered so far; enough of the right foods so that muscles have adequate fuel; plenty of oxygen coursing through your lungs and tissues; the right mix of pleasure activities for your personal tastes; the right shoes and clothes for what you are doing; the right time and place; and perhaps things like the right music to boost your psychic energies. Physical activity, like eating, is intended to be an enjoyable thing. If it has not been so for you, you need to identify the things which are blocking this most pleasurable dimension of life for you – and dump them.

As you grow used to using your body for a higher

level of energy output, so your capacity for pleasure will grow. As you become more competent you will get that buzz that draws you on to do more, or to do it again. This sort of positive feedback is experienced by many people only in sexual activity, but any physical person knows that the same sort of pleasurable bodily rewards happen at many levels with other sorts of activity. Of course, being more physically competent will improve your sex life; this is the way positive cycles work. The more you do, the more you will be able to do, and the more you will want to do. When you get more from your body, you will appreciate yourself more. Your capacity for all types of output increases and so your opportunities for pleasure increase; you may begin to recognise within yourself the potential for development in totally unexpected directions. You will have launched yourself into a cycle of enrichment that offers multiple benefits.

Many of us reach adulthood with fixed ideas about ourselves and our abilities which limit what we do and block half-hearted resolutions to change. Remember Arabella's story. To change, Arabella had to throw out those beliefs that were not working for her and look instead for truths that helped her to recognise and develop her real nature.

Today, she has a wider range of physical skills and more energy than she would have imagined possible. And life is far more fun! But before she could move into this wider, more exciting world she had to junk her low-energy fat-person ideas. She had to start eating properly, get her metabolic rate up, become more active, get her body working right. Now she can appreciate herself as she never could when ideas like 'I can't ride a bike', 'I don't run', 'I can't hit balls', 'I can't dance', 'I don't like sport', 'I mustn't eat', 'I'm fat', controlled her leisure hours.

How much do you need to change? How high are your metabolic fires burning? Try the following questionnaire to find out.

Metabolic Rate Questionnaire

1. *Have you been dieting, continuously or at intervals?*
   a. Yes, for 6 months or more
   b. Yes, for 1 to 6 months
   c. Not strictly on a diet, but consciously controlling calorie intake for more than a year

2. *Have you recently been on a very low-calorie or low-carbohydrate diet?*
   a. Yes, similar to the Cambridge diet or equivalent
   b. Other low-carbohydrate diets (similar to the Scarsdale)

3. *Have you found that you gain weight on very little food?*
   a. Yes, absolutely; I eat like the proverbial bird
   b. Yes, I think so   c. Not sure or no

4. *Do you seem to feel the cold more than most people?*
   a. Yes, always   b. Sometimes

5. *Do you tire more easily than your friends?*
   a. Yes, always   b. Sometimes

6. *Would you describe your build as muscular or sturdy (mesomorphic)?*
   a. Yes, definitely   c. Definitely not
   b. Not especially

Scoring

1. a6 b3 c3   4. a4 b2
2. a6 b3   5. a4 b2
3. a4 b2 c0   6. a0 b0 c4

Sum your total for this section for your Metabolic Rate Score. Men should subtract 6 from this total because they have a higher proportion of muscle and a naturally higher metabolic rate than women.

Over 18
You have a very low metabolic rate. Your body runs very economically, like a car with a tiny engine. You find it difficult to speed up, to summon up energy and to avoid laying down fat. Some people have the inbuilt ability to drop their metabolic rate very quickly in response to food shortages; these are the people whose ancestors were particularly good at surviving starvation. By subjecting yourself to famine conditions you have set off this protective mechanism – and you will set it off again every time you go hungry. The body learns to react faster and more dramatically each time the starvation cycle comes around.

You are going to have to accept that some weight gain may occur before you can shed that fat effectively. Do not panic. Just understand that you must persuade your body that there is no need to hang on to fat stores, because food is plentiful. You are going to eat well from now on.

You must eat much more complex carbohydrate (bread, potatoes, rice, muesli, pasta) and protein foods (nuts, fish, eggs, lean meat). Use the energy this food gives you to increase your activity level.

8–18
Your metabolic rate is low but you should be able to recover to high energy levels within a few months. Using the knowledge that you now have, consider what aspects of your life need to change so that you can move to a higher energy level. Do you need to unlock doors that your assumptions about yourself have kept closed for years? Perhaps you need to devote more time and attention to yourself and your health requirements. This would be time well spent because it will make you capable of more.

Under 8
Your problems are not due to an inherently low meta- bolic rate so you should find it relatively easy to persuade

your body to shed excess fat. Chapter Nine will guide you on your way. Always be sure you choose the right type of food, eat when you're hungry, and take care to avoid chemicals, drugs and allergens that add to your weight problems.

Whatever your score, the following chapters will guide you on to the right track for you to EAT YOURSELF THIN.

Summary

- Women should eat frequent small meals. Men may do better on less frequent larger meals.
- Eating more good food will create a new metabolic profile – that of a slim person.

Action Now

- ○ *Eat a good breakfast every day; include a free-range egg, sugar-free cereal with skimmed milk, or both.*
- ○ *Gradually increase your intake of good food.*
- ○ *Break chocolate, coffee and junk food addictions.*
- ○ *Begin breathing exercises (Appendix B).*
- ○ *If you believe you don't like being physically active – think again! Think of different activities that you might enjoy and find out about them.*

CHAPTER 8

Phase Three – Burn Fat

IN THIS PHASE you will be using your well-nourished body and the energy it produces to shed fat permanently. You will be changing your body composition, from its present mixture of fat and lean tissue, to one which has a greater predominance of lean. This means your *shape* will be changing, and you must be prepared to make the most of this opportunity.

The obsession with weight among fat people is based on two things. First, weight is easy to measure and bureaucrats, in medicine or in businesses like insurance, like things that are easy to measure. When averaged out over thousands of people such measurements may have meaning, but for the individual they are more a source of misery than helpful guidance. Second, they allow diet merchants to prove they are good – look how many pounds you have lost, no matter that it is water or lean tissue – or that you are bad – look, you have gained pounds, you have not stuck to the diet. It doesn't matter that dieting inevitably makes you fatter.

As your final rejection of fat-person behaviour, you should by now have thrown your scales away. Your full-length mirror is both a treat and a necessity, because the only way you can monitor your changing shape is by looking at yourself. In your mirror you will see your new creation; you will watch dimples and folds disappear and enjoy the emergence of firm curves.

You are embarking on the discriminate loss of flesh. It is another crucial difference between the EAT YOURSELF THIN strategy and that of conventional dieting. By following our suggestions you will shed fat selectively and gain firm lean mass where you need it. The underlying difference is reflected in the results. Dieters passively put on fat while losing lean; you will actively lose fat while creating healthy lean. You will not turn bulgy and muscular, unless you work hard at it using body-building techniques. You are however likely to gain some lean mass where it will improve your shape, for example on your back and shoulders, and perhaps accentuate the shape of your legs. You will also gain unseen lean tissue by increasing the size and capacity of some vital organs, particularly your heart and liver.

You should welcome this increase in lean tissue mass. It will add to your general health and vitality, and perhaps of more immediate importance, it will help you burn fat. It is lean tissue that burns fat; the higher your proportion of lean tissue the more fat you can burn, and when you are thin it will be easier to remain that way. So anything which encourages the change from fat to lean should be welcomed. A larger liver will improve your metabolism and increase your detoxification capacity, making you less prone to deposit unwanted substances into fat. And a bigger, healthier heart will make you more vital and increase life expectancy.

So, for the last time, forget the *quantity* of flesh you are carrying, and concentrate on its *quality* instead. Get in front of your mirror, feel the muscles on your arms and legs. Are they firm and near the surface? Feel your skin; is it smooth and supple? Feel around your waist and tummy. Are there loose folds of flesh there? Try taking a pinch of that abdominal fat: can you find more than an inch between your thumb and forefinger at any point? If so, read on – you don't need to know any more than that to guide you to appropriate action.

Basic Activity

The first and most important activity for everyone is walking. Human beings are designed to do a lot of walking. It is the most natural activity, one that is common to both sexes and all ages and body types. Whether you currently see yourself as fit or feeble, you should walk every day, as far and as briskly as you can.

It is sensible to *average* at least 2 miles a day; that's half an hour, walking at a reasonable pace. Until you get used to the distance and pace, measure out 2 miles on a large-scale map of your district and try it several times. You can use the map to explore interesting parts you may not have reached before.

With these relatively short walks, a brisk and constant pace is the best way to mobilise fat. Leave all your bits and pieces at home, and avoid restrictive clothing, hold your head up high, breathe deeply, relax your shoulders and get a spring in your step. Make your stride long enough to feel you are stretching your legs. Traditional kerb stones are handy pace-makers; try keeping in step with them. Don't slip into a stroll, be definite about it.

You will feel the effects quite quickly as the increased energy demand warms your body and you have to peel off layers of excess clothing – set out prepared for this eventuality! If you are very over-fat, completely unaccustomed to applying yourself to physical activity or getting on in years, or any combination of these, take it easy at first; do what you think you can manage, and see how you feel the next day. If you are OK, do more; if you feel the strain a bit, miss a day and then do a little less. Build up slowly; the idea is to train, not to strain.

Treat walking as an everyday background activity, and make it a natural part of your life. You are not aiming to get any great charge from it, although if you find it a novel activity, it may also bring exhilaration until you acclimatise. This regular activity, with a brisk free-swinging action designed to carry you along, will ensure that you will never completely lose fitness even if more energetic activity becomes erratic for any reason.

The great advantage of walking is that you are extremely unlikely to overstrain yourself. Walking will build you up *and* fine you down, naturally. If you invest in a pair of good shoes or trainers such as Hi-Tec Silver Shadows, which are cheap and good for both walking and running, you should not get sore feet or blisters.

The rationale for the apparently mundane suggestion

of walking is that long walks are ideal for burning fat at a steady rate. When you are doing a Sunday walk of 4 hours or more, putting continual demand on your system, your fat problem could be solved.

While walking is the type of activity which will burn off fat very effectively, it does have a major drawback. Because it is so natural to our physiology we adjust to it very readily; so it has little effect on your metabolic rate (unless you become a Sunday walk fanatic). In practical terms this means that while walking is a very safe and sure way of shedding fat, it may be rather slow and it may not allow you to develop the sort of energy levels and food intake you would ideally like.

If you are in good health and want to burn fat when not actually exercising, you will need to push your metabolic rate up higher. To do this you will have to build some more demanding activities on top of your basic walking. You will have to get into the realms of greater physical activity, of harder exercise. Sounds grim? Not if you do it right! Remember the pleasure principle; true, most pleasure comes with effort, and generally the greater the effort, the greater the pleasure; but we are not interested in aches and pains or anything even mildly approaching agony. The secret is to build up slowly so that, as well as enjoying whatever you are doing, you are increasing your capacity to do more. If you over-stretch yourself, your body will deny you the pleasure and give you pain instead. There is another sound reason for avoiding aching muscles; aches mean there is a build-up of lactic acid which will inhibit the release of fat. That is clearly not to your advantage.

The objective is to build up the enzyme systems that make the mitochondria work. And by using your body, you increase the number of mitochondria and the lipo-protein lipases that release fat from store, so that you can use more fat with the glycogen from your food. Muscles will only burn fat when they are working efficiently, so although you will have to train them to improve their capacity, you should not overdo it in the mistaken belief that if it feels bad it is good for you. When you are working within your capacity, you will burn more fat and thus create more capacity.

So whatever vigorous activity you go for, never go for the burn and forget 'pain means gain' (or weight loss). Disregard all that masochistic nonsense. Go for pleasure every time; it is your body's way of telling you you are doing the right thing! Of course, getting the judgement right so that you don't slip over from enough to too much will take some time. Sometimes you may have to push yourself a little to get yourself going, but at other times you will be enjoying your activity so much that you won't want to stop. You are learning about yourself, so if you do overdo it and have one or two stiff or aching days, chalk it up to experience; it happens to all of us.

One way to add to your pleasure during activity is with music to lift and carry you along. Dance, a primal human recreation, combines activity and music in ways appealing to almost everyone. Your movements can be slow and exploratory or driving and dynamic, to suit your mood and needs, and excellent exercise, not just for the body, but for the mind and spirit as well.

Whatever activity you choose to use up your increased energy and burn off fat, food can be used to both stimulate and help you rest and recover afterwards, while fat is still being metabolised. The general rules are that you should eat proteins for activation, and complex carbohydrates for relaxation and general sustenance. That may sound like the opposite of what is generally believed; quite right, but we are doing the opposite of what generally happens, shedding fat rather than accumulating it.

Most of your meals should be firmly based on complex carbohydrates, but you will raise the rate at which your body burns fat if the last meal before an activity session is high in protein and low in carbohydrate. This is because protein stimulates your body to produce a hormone which speeds up the fat-burning process. Make sure you allow time for digestion; the more strenuous you are going to be, the longer you should allow.

If you like to exercise first thing in the morning, you may only want a drink and perhaps some fruit beforehand, with breakfast following later. Be careful if pre-breakfast activity kills your appetite. You will be hungry by mid-morning; this is where those fruit, nut and seed, and raw vegetable snacks should be at hand.

You should eat protein at breakfast if you plan a strenuous pre-lunch session. Grapefruit, an egg, a portion of kedgeree perhaps, and just one slice of toast, would be suitable – but have more if you wish! If you are going to be active in the afternoon, have that sort of menu at lunchtime and have a breakfast of grains. Toast, porridge, sugar-free muesli, shredded wheat, or any other sugar-free cereal with skimmed milk or yoghurt, and fruit, should set you up. Fill up for a physically demanding evening with protein and vegetables and save your carbohydrate for a late-night snack.

When relaxing, go for complex carbohydrates. A low protein, high carbohydrate supper will help you relax by raising the level of the brain hormone serotonin which is necessary for sleep.

Understanding Exercise

To get the type and timing of exercise right to achieve your individual purpose as effectively as possible, you need to understand about exercise. The following considerations will help you with your personal schedule.

The Warm-up

Warming up before exercise is mandatory. You should never subject your body to any strenuous activity without first warming up to get the systems turned on and running. When you are ready, you will feel warm.

The warm-up is important to loosen your muscles, ligaments and joints so that you do not injure yourself. It prepares your heart and lungs for sustained effort and initiates the changes in your hormone systems that will maximise the benefit of your exertions. After strenuous activity, shake out and loosen up to wind down. Emergency starts and stops are for emergencies only.

Breathing
Learning to breathe effectively is very important. It may seem strange, but it can be easy to forget to breathe when you are concentrating on movement; yet without sufficient oxygen your muscles cannot function properly. Breathe in when you're making expansive movements, thrusting your arms or legs away from your body; breathe out when your limbs come in towards the body. Always breathe as slowly and as deeply as you can. That way you absorb more of the oxygen from each breath and get rid of more of your unwanted carbon dioxide. You will find that you can, for example, run further with less effort by breathing slowly and consciously curbing the desire to pant.

Give Yourself Time
Your body takes some time to adapt to exercise and achieve the changes you want. You should exercise for at least 20 minutes in each session, which means you need at least half an hour: 5 minutes to change and warm up, 5 minutes for a quick shower or towel-down before you change back. Unless you are super-efficient, 40 minutes is more realistic. The longer you can make your session last, the more effective it will be.

Do not be afraid to take rests during your exercise session. When you have used up the immediately available glycogen in your muscles, you may have to wait a few moments for your liver to shunt more fuel through. If activity makes your muscles begin to bind up and fail to respond, take a break, shake them loose and stroll about. Do not collapse or sit, keep moving gently; you will recover faster.

Lasting Change Takes Time!
Do not expect athletic brilliance within a month; but neither should you give up on yourself. If you start to

lose heart or imagine you're too old to succeed, remember some of the people who have taken up marathon running: Madge Sharples joined a running club after her husband died, to take her mind off her grief. She is now in her *seventies* and still running marathons! Priscilla Welch, who started jogging in her late thirties, won the New York marathon at the age of forty-two.

You must have patience. By exploiting the understandable desire for instant transformation, crash diet pundits have implanted the expectation that large amounts of fat can be shed very quickly and passively. As you realise, the situation is not that simple and the costs of quick weight loss outweigh the benefits. Although our system does make rapid fat loss possible, it may not happen until you've been following it for a while. If you persist and work at it patiently, this method *will* succeed and the fat loss will be permanent.

Even if the slim body takes some time to emerge, the glow of health should develop quickly and perceptibly over the course of your first month. Observe the changes as they happen: watch your skin become smoother and more elastic; watch the new life in your hair, the roses appearing in your cheeks. These are the first signs of success. With these signs will come more energy and vitality; you will be building success on success.

Throw Yourself Into It!
Do not be afraid to use your body. Gentle pottering is a waste of time. You have to get your systems fired up, get your heart-rate up and, without straining, keep it up. If you do not, your body will not respond by increasing metabolic rate and energy output. Mental commitment is important; make up your mind you are going to do it and do not be half-hearted.

Lack of Motivation
If you feel listless when activity time draws near, if you feel that general disinclination for work of any kind that used to sell patent medicines, stop and think about it. It

may be your subconscious saying 'Are you sure?', perhaps because your body needs its energy for some other purpose of which you are unaware.

Try listening to up-beat music and start bopping or bouncing to shake things into place. After a few minutes your mood will probably change and you will be ready to go. But be aware of problems beyond mood: you could be tired, under attack from infection or emotionally drained. A slow bath and bed might be the most appropriate action. *Never* stress yourself when fighting infection; wait until the battle is won, then go on.

Nobody can tell you precisely what is right for you at any particular time; you have to tune into your own needs, make judgements yourself. In general terms, the more you do, the more you are likely to benefit, but if you push yourself beyond your capacity at any time, you will slip back and you could put your health at risk.

Encouragement
Exercising with someone else can be the best way to keep going when motivation flags. It is unlikely that you will both feel 'off' at the same time. Exercising together opens up the prospect of playing games such as badminton and tennis, which are fun and good for burning fat. You could join a local sports or athletic club; even if you never make the A team, the enthusiasm and acceptance of those around you will carry you forward. In athletic clubs, you get the benefit of social activity as well as advice and training facilities.

Use Your Largest Muscles
The larger the muscle group you use, the more energy and fat you can burn. Our largest muscles are in the thighs, so anything that relies on leg power uses the biggest fat-burners. This is why walking, running, dancing, skipping, cycling and rowing are so beneficial.

Achieving the Shape You Desire
How far you will be able to reshape your body to match

your ideal depends on two factors: your genetic make-up and the amount of effort you're able to devote to yourself. We are all born with potential to develop in certain ways, but only some of this potential will be realised. As you change to a thin lifestyle, new aspects of your physical potential will appear. You might find that you had the potential for the most gorgeous shapely shoulders – but it never got expressed because you didn't use your arms enough for the muscles to develop. Or you might discover that a marvellous hourglass figure was potentially there under layers of fat, but you never lived the way that allowed it to emerge. By adopting the EAT YOURSELF THIN strategy you create the possibility of expressing your best features.

Unfortunately, genetics can block some of our fantasies! You will never have long limbs if you weren't designed that way; so while you may look attractive, with waist and hips as slim as you want them to be, you cannot expect fashion model proportions and you will only make yourself miserable if you aim for that sort of ideal. What we each have to discover is the best possible shape for ourselves to achieve, the best way that we can develop our individual potential. Aim to become the most magnificent form of what you are.

The precise effects of exercise training will depend on your genetic make-up. Some people will build relatively large muscles easily; these are the mesomorphs, the stocky, muscular types. The brilliant German tennis player, Steffi Graf, has a mesomorphic build, as has Daley Thompson; but the differences in hormones between the sexes mean that men build heavier muscles than women, even if both work equally hard. Ectomorphs have relatively long, narrow bodies whatever training they do; they are the best jumpers and long-distance runners. Endomorphic types are bulky; heavyweight people, they are designed for heavyweight activities like weight-lifting and throwing.

Endomorphs and mesomorphs tend to run readily to fat if they don't use their bodies enough. You probably

have strong endomorphic and/or mesomorphic com-
ponents in your body type or you would not be reading
this book! The EAT YOURSELF THIN system will work best
for mesomorphs, though its principles are appropriate
for all body types. Mesomorphs predominate in northern
latitudes where our ancestors had to be strong to
survive. But whatever your body type, you have plenty
of options for reshaping!

Slimming and Refining
To refine your body and reduce bulk, you should concentrate on light loads and fast movements. This means
that you should move quickly. To get the coordination
right for complex movements, learn them like new dance
steps: start off slowly and speed up once you have got it
right. To slim the body, you should continue light exercise for long sessions, using maximum oxygen intake to
burn glycogen and fat.

Adding Shape
If you need more flesh to add shape to any part of your
body, you should use heavier activities such as weight-
training to develop the underlying muscles. The principle is to use heavy loads with few repetitions; this is
anaerobic activity, which cannot be continued for long.
Repeat the exercise every 2 or 3 days. Examples of
suitable activities for muscle-building include press-ups
to improve the pectoral muscles behind the breasts,
weight-lifting to improve the shape of back and shoulders, squats and sprints to develop leg muscles. Warming
up is particularly important before this sort of activity.

Anaerobic and Aerobic Activities
Anaerobic activities are defined as those that demand
more oxygen than you can absorb during the exercise;
they set up an 'oxygen debt', such that you continue to
breathe hard to recover for some time after you have
stopped. Aerobic activities are less strenuous; you should
be able to get sufficient oxygen to continue for a long

time without running out of breath. Anaerobic activities are strenuous and can cause problems if you try to do them before you're ready; gentler, aerobic activities are safe. Walking is aerobic; it is totally beneficial and very unlikely to overstress any part of your body. Shedding fat fast requires more intense exercise but you should be cautious until you know your limits.

There is no hard line between the anaerobic and aerobic exercise. When we move relatively slower over the ground, we call it walking, which is aerobic; move a bit faster, trot or jog, and this too is aerobic unless you're not used to exercise. Running is aerobic if you are fit, but anaerobic if you are not and you find it a struggle. Fast running (sprinting) is always anaerobic because nobody can keep it up for long. So the point at which aerobic exercise becomes anaerobic depends on your level of fitness. What is anaerobic for you today could be aerobic in a couple of months' time, when you are more accustomed to it. Discriminate between aerobic and anaerobic activities by focussing on your breathing: if you can get in enough air to keep going for 10 minutes or more without stopping to pant and recover, your activity is aerobic; if you run out of breath quickly, your activity is anaerobic.

Getting the Best of Both Worlds
If you want to get the maximum benefit from an exercise session or to achieve the fastest re-shaping possible by exercising every day, you should mix anaerobic and aerobic activities. Alternate strenuous demanding anaerobic routines with lighter, aerobic ones which help your muscles to recover. Vigorous activities such as sprinting, weight-lifting, fast hilly walks, rowing and swimming can alternate with shorter walks, cycling, rhythmic dancing or floor exercises. Light exercise helps your body to deal with the products of heavy workouts, while heavy exercise enhances the fat-burning potential of light exercise. Do not try to push yourself too hard – always remember the pleasure principle!

Everyday Activities
Do not overlook the possibility of burning fat through everyday activities. If you use your new energy and muscle power instead of power tools, many daily activities can become valuable in your life as a slim person. Sawing logs is an excellent form of exercise, perhaps for a privileged minority; but anyone can knead bread dough, dig a garden or allotment to produce organic food, or run upstairs; and how about massaging your partner or friends and getting a massage in return?

Energy Use
If you feel you have more energy than you are using, speed things up. When you increase the speed at which you carry out any activity, the energy demand is increased greatly. Going twice as fast does not demand twice the energy: in fact, energy used in movement is a cubic function, which uses $2 \times 2 \times 2$, or 8 times the energy when you double the speed! So you will quickly notice the effects of any increase in speed.

Keeping Going
If you feel muscles beginning to tire but you want to do more, use a different set of muscles. Working different muscles groups, perhaps changing from leg to arm exercises when your legs begin to tire, will not only enhance fat-burning but it will actually help the tired muscles to recover. If you are doing something which occupies the whole body, like running or rowing, the only thing to do is change gear. Slow down and change the length or speed of your stride or stroke.

If you exercise long and hard enough, you will experience the athlete's 'high'. Your brain reacts by producing beta-endorphins, neuro-hormones which can make you feel wonderful – calm and alert, or else euphoric, with a heightened sense of energy and reduced sense of pain. Many regular runners become addicted to the effects of these naturally produced euphorics. You will experience these effects when your body is accustomed to exercise;

do not strain yourself to produce them, they will come naturally when you are ready.

Addiction and Obsession

Either because of addiction to the athlete's high, or because of obsessive fear of fatness, some people exercise too much and damage their health. Very frequent and intensive exercise combined with inadequate food can cause disturbances in hormone balance which makes the bones become brittle. The warning signal for women is when their periods cease – a common experience among young dancers and gymnasts who work their bodies very hard indeed. If your periods stop when you are neither pregnant nor menopausal, ask yourself if you could be getting dangerously thin. Be honest. If the answer could possibly be yes, you must redress the balance; eat more and exercise less.

Hunger

Exercise can make you feel more hungry *or* reduce your appetite! You will find that your appetite fits your nutrient needs more precisely when you adopt an active lifestyle. Never exercise when you feel hungry; eat instead. An hour or so after exercise, when your body rightly expects a reward, eat meals based on complex carbohydrates such as potatoes, brown bread, brown rice, pasta and vegetables to aid rest and recuperation.

Fluid Loss

Always drink plenty of pure water when you exercise. Do not believe that sweat, or water loss, is the same as fat loss: that is an old diet con. Drink! It is easy to become dehydrated when you are sweating and water is necessary to help your body cope with the waste products of burning fat. If the waste system cannot cope, fat will stop moving. Tea and coffee are not as beneficial as water because they are diuretics; they stimulate further water loss and can actually increase dehydration.

Toxic Reactions
If you start to feel unwell during your activity session or during the subsequent 24 hours, you may be experiencing a toxic reaction, caused by overloading your liver. Common symptoms include headache, dizziness, nausea, and general non-specific malaise. Some people feel depressed the day after exercise; this can also be a symptom of liver overload. If you suspect that you are suffering delayed reactions to exercise, keep a diary and record your health and moods. You will be able to pick up any pattern quite quickly.

Toxic reactions should never be ignored. Stop exercising if you become nauseous or develop a pounding headache. Drink plenty of water and rest. Treat delayed reactions with a diet rich in fruit and fresh vegetables and by conscientiously avoiding tea, coffee, alcohol, cigarettes and all potential causes of chemical stress.

Nutrient imbalance or deficiencies increase the risk of toxic reactions. Zinc, sulphur-containing amino acids (see page 59) and vitamin C are particularly important. If you find you often feel unwell after exercise, make sure your diet contains enough of these crucial nutrients by increasing your intake of rich dietary sources.

Toxic reactions are particularly common when you try to lose fat which accumulated rapidly during your exposure to heavy chemical load. The most common situation is when you put on fat in response to drug therapy; that fat may be heavily contaminated with drug metabolites that your liver was unable to handle. Many medicines, including anti-depressants, tranquillisers, and hormone-related drugs such as oral contraceptives, can produce this sort of effect. Our book, *Persistent Fat and How to Lose It* (Century-Hutchinson) gives you a list of drugs known to be associated with weight gain and explains how to cope with the whole problem of toxic overload and limited liver capacity.

Menstrual Problems
Changing your diet to that recommended in previous

chapters and increasing your activity levels will have a marked positive effect on problems such as PMT and period pain. Your metabolic functions are linked with your menstrual cycle; each affects the other.

The best time for fat-burning is the first half of the month, from the beginning of your period until ovulation, while muscle-building is more effective during the second half of the month. Use the time before ovulation for fat loss and you will be working with the natural effects of your hormones; concentrate on adding lean tissue after ovulation. As your activity levels increase, you will find that hormone fluctuations even out and your periods are likely to become lighter and less troublesome.

Summary

- When you lose fat and gain lean, your body shape and function improves and your metabolic rate rises.
- Lean tissue burns fat and keeps you slim.
- Walking is the safest way to burn fat.
- Build harder exercise into your life slowly – it will raise your metabolic rate but you must ease into it.
- Eat protein to aid fat mobilisation, and carbo-hydrate for relaxation, recouperation and general sustenance.

Action Now

- ○ *Make time for activity – it should be an important part of your daily life.*
- ○ *Walk as briskly as you can for 2 miles every day.*
- ○ *If you find walking easy, go for a long hike once a week.*
- ○ *Start practising the warm-up routine (page 171).*
- ○ *Remember the pleasure principle in activity!*

CHAPTER 9

Action Plans

THE EAT YOURSELF THIN system offers three Action Plans to suit different needs: Fast Track, Happy Medium and Long Haul. Each aims to increase metabolic rate by using plenty of good food and high oxygen consumption to sustain an active life. You can select the right plan for your body type and circumstances with help from the questionnaire on page 103. When you begin your Action Plan, you should be eating a balanced diet of high-quality fresh food and walking every day.

First, we will outline the three Action Plans.

You will burn fat quickly on the **Fast Track**, but you have to be fairly fit to cope with it. Do not try to push yourself onto the Fast Track unless you are sure you are ready for it; it is possible to overload your system and make yourself ill by launching yourself into a heavy exercise schedule before your body is able to adjust. If you score over 25 on the questionnaire at the end of this section, you should not embark on the Fast Track; doing too much, too fast could delay your arrival at your desired goal.

If you are fit, healthy, relatively young, and have only a moderate amount of excess fat, the Fast Track will allow you to trim down quickly. This is the EAT YOURSELF THIN equivalent of the crash diet – but it doesn't produce gruesome fat gain if you stop doing it! It demands discipline in both eating and exercise patterns, but if it's the right track for you, it will make you look and feel marvellous very quickly. It requires that you walk for at least half an hour every day and that you do more vigorous exercise for a further half hour, 5 days a week. At the weekend, you will need to allow at least 2 hours for a long walk. This makes a total of **7 hours a week** devoted to exercise.

This level of activity demands a consistently high nutrient intake and you will have to take special care to protect yourself from the effects of anti-nutrients and pollution. When you are burning fat fast, your detoxification systems will be working at full stretch and you should not take any risks with your health.

You should be able to lose all your excess flab within **3 months** on this Action Plan. After that, you may be a convert to a high-energy lifestyle and just want to stay very active! More likely, you will opt for a maintenance level of activity that keeps you in balance once your goal has been achieved.

Most people will be happiest on the **Happy Medium**. Some will start on Happy Medium, find they can go faster and move onto the more demanding Fast Track if they wish; others may find it over-ambitious and change to the more comfortable Long Haul, which will take them to the same destination by a gentler route.

The Happy Medium Plan will push your metabolic rate up gradually. It is right for people who are in fairly good health and who can devote a moderate amount of time to activity, or who need more time to adjust their lifestyles. The advantage of Happy Medium is that it is only moderately demanding so it suits those who are holding down stressful jobs or struggling to cope with the demands of everyday life. Eating well and deep breathing are important but the activity component is relatively more relaxing and less strenuous. You will need to plan for at least three half-hour exercise sessions each week, in addition to your daily walk and a longer weekend walk. Allow a total of about **5 to 6 hours a week**, but you'll probably find that the walking component of this can be fitted easily into your daily life.

We anticipate that most people will need **6 to 12 months** on Happy Medium to lose excess fat and train their metabolisms to function at a level that will keep them looking and feeling good. It's not a long time to gain the far-reaching benefits that you will enjoy.

The **Long Haul** Action Plan involves gradual progressive training over a longer period. It is suitable for those who are very over-fat, unfit or getting on in years. Many people who start on the Long Haul will be able to move up to Happy Medium as their health and fitness improves. Long Haul activities are not strenuous but require regular exercise sessions to build up capacity gradually. Allow about **four to five hours a week**.

The Long Haul will induce your body to shed excess fat progressively and safely, though it may not involve sufficient physiological demand to turn you into a slim person. If you fall into one of the groups for whom we recommend this gradual approach, you will find that your health improves in a range of important ways. You can expect, for example, that your blood pressure will become normal if it has been high; that your blood sugar will become more even; your emotions will be more stable; your energy levels will rise and you will sleep better at night.

People over the age of sixty should normally expect to stay with the Long Haul. Rapid fat loss is particularly unwise for older people because they are especially susceptible to illness and injury if they overstress their detoxification systems or push themselves too hard without allowing adequate time for recuperation. The body heals and rebuilds itself more slowly as the years accumulate; little but often is the key to success.

Which Action Plan? Do this questionnaire to find out ...

1. *How many excess pounds do you consider you are carrying?*
   a. Fewer than 15   c. 25 to 40
   b. 15 to 25   d. Over 40

2. *How old are you?*
   a. Under 30   d. 50 to 60
   b. 30 to 40   e. Over 60
   c. 40 to 50

3. *Do you suffer from any of the following? (Check all that apply to you.)*
   a. Hypertension (high blood pressure)
   b. Arthritis
   c. Angina or other heart symptoms
   d. Poor liver function[1]
   e. Asthma, colitis or chronic allergic illness
   f. Any chronic debilitating infection
   g. Breathlessness (apart from during exercise)

4. *Were you fat throughout childhood and adolescence?*
   a. Not significantly   c. Yes, always fat
   b. Fat at times only

5. *Have you been dieting in the last six months?*
   a. Yes, most or all of the time
   b. Yes, intermittently
   c. Not strictly dieting, but I eat very little
   d. No

6. *Do you react to strenuous exercise in any of the following ways. (Check all that apply to you.)*
   a. Nausea, at the time or later
   b. Headaches
   c. Urgent need to use the lavatory
   d. Muscle or joint pain lasting three days or more
   e. Chest pain
   f. Increased libido
   g. Don't know – I don't do strenuous exercise

7. *Check which of the following items apply to you.*
   a. Pregnant
   b. Breastfeeding
   c. Have you given birth in the last four months?
   d. Have you had a major surgical operation in the past year?
   e. None of the above

8. *Which of the following do you consider your usual activity level to be?*
   a. Significantly higher than average
   b. Average or slightly above average
   c. Probably below average
   d. Very low

9. *What do you feel your usual energy level is?*
   a. Very high – you have lots of go!
   b. Acceptably high, you have enough energy to do what you want
   c. Rather low, you are frequently tired
   d. Dismally low

10. *How would you describe your basic body shape (under the fat!)?*
   a. Stocky and muscular
   b. Big in relation to your height but not muscular
   c. Average: you don't fit any extreme type
   d. Delicate or willowy

11. *How is your excess fat distributed?*
   a. Mainly around the waist, belly and back
   b. All over the body, quite evenly
   c. Mainly on the hips, buttocks and thighs

12. *How many hours per week do you spend watching TV, reading novels, or in other forms of passive recreation? (Don't guess the answer to this: re-run your last week in your mind and add up the hours.)*
   a. Fewer than 4 hours
   b. 4 to 8 hours
   c. More than 8 hours

13. *Do you take regular exercise?*
   a. Yes – I exercise hard for an hour or more every week
   b. Yes – I take gentle exercise (eg swimming, cycling) for an hour or more each week
   c. I exercise erratically, some weeks for more than an hour, other weeks hardly at all
   d. I take less than an hour's exercise each week
   e. My work involves considerable physical activity
   f. I don't go in for exercise

14. *Do you use any of the following drugs every day?*
   a. Steroids
   b. Beta-blockers
   c. Analgesics (pain-killers)

Scoring

Add the scores for each question according to the key below.
1. a1 b2 c4 d5
2. a1 b3 c6 d9 e12
3. Add the following scores for the conditions you suffer:
   a3 b4 c7 d5 e3 f5 g5
4. a1 b2 c3
5. a4 b2 c3 d1
6. Add the following scores for all reactions you experience:
   a6 b4 c2 d3 e8 f0 g6
7. a4 b6 c3 d4 e0
8. a1 b2 c3 d5
9. a0 b2 c4 d5
10. a0 b2 c2 d3
11. a4 b2 c1
12. a2 b1 c3
13. a0 b2 c3 d4 e5 f2
14. Add 8 to your score for any drug on this list. (This is for your protection; if you are taking any of these medicines regularly, your health problems will tend to reduce your exercise tolerance.)

[1] If you've had hepatitis, jaundice or other liver disease you should assume your liver function is poor; also if alcohol, solvents and chemicals readily make you ill.

Add together your total scores for each question and now find out your rate.

First, however, a warning. Use your questionnaire results for guidance only. No questionnaire of this type can discriminate perfectly between people who would be best suited to each of the Action Plans; if your circumstances are unusual, you may not fit the usual pattern. In the final analysis, you must use your own judgement to assess your capacity for exercise. Nevertheless, you should take a high score seriously because it means that fast fat loss could be hazardous for you.

Under 24
You are already quite fit and you have developed the potential that will allow you to increase your fitness so you can take the Fast Track if you choose. If you are in any doubt about your ability, however, try Happy Medium for a couple of weeks to build up your capacity before launching into the high-energy Fast Track.

25 to 34
You are in the Happy Medium category. You have some problems that could make the Fast Track risky, but you have the capacity for a higher energy lifestyle. As health problems disappear with your rising level of fitness, try the questionnaire again to see if you're ready for the Fast Track.

35 to 44
You are not yet sufficiently fit to shed fat quickly but you should make good progress with the Happy Medium Action Plan. You will shed fat steadily until you are as slim as you want to be and you will learn how to live so that you stay slim permanently.

Over 44
Start on the Long Haul. You may find that this is the best routine for you to adopt indefinitely; it's a healthy way of life that will gradually trim away any excess fat. If you're determined to get thinner faster, try the questionnaire again after a month on Long Haul see if you're ready for Happy Medium. If your score is still high, continue building up your health on the Long Haul; use the questionnaire to re-check when you feel your fitness and energy levels have improved.

Whatever Action Plan you select, pin this memo on your wall:

> TRAIN NOT STRAIN
> QUALITY NOT QUANTITY
> NO EMERGENCY STOPS OR STARTS
> WATCH FOR LIVER OVERLOAD
>
> REMEMBER THE PLEASURE PRINCIPLE!

1. Fast Track Action Plan

Warning: The Fast Track is suitable only for people in good health. Do not start on it if you scored 25 or more on the questionnaire in this chapter. If you have any illness or are under medical supervision for any reason, check with your doctor before you attempt the Fast Track.

Fast Track Diet
To set your metabolism for maximum energy output, you should be eating plenty of nutritious food in frequent small meals. Eat fresh, high-quality foods to minimise toxin load and maximise nutrient intake. Increase your food intake gradually as your activity levels rise. Your dietary priorities are these:

1. Eat as much complex carbohydrate as you want to keep energy levels high and avoid hunger. Go for potatoes, wholemeal bread, rice, pasta, peas and beans.

2. Avoid fats as far as possible, except those found naturally in foods such as fish, nuts and eggs. Take advantage of meals based on brown rice, pasta or potatoes which don't require added fat to make them palatable. Snack on rice cakes or sandwiches; choose banana or other low-fat sandwich fillings. When eating out, ask for baked potato with as little butter as possible, fish, and salads with minimal dressing.

3. Ensure high intake of zinc, iron, vitamin C, sulphur-containing amino acids and essential fatty acids by eating plenty of fresh nuts, free-range eggs, fish, red kidney beans, salads, citrus and berry fruits, organically produced liver and dark turkey meat.

4. Be especially careful to avoid processed and fried foods.

5. If you can't stop counting calories, aim for about 2,000 daily (men: 2,500) on Week 1, progressing to 2,400 to 3,000 (men: 3,100 to 3,800) from Week 3 onwards when your activity levels are higher. But remember: *these calories must come from nutrient-rich food* – not sugar, processed food or alcohol. See menu suggestions, pages 162–66.

Fast Track Activity Schedule

Preparation
Make a list of your preferred activities and equip yourself with the right clothing, partners, venues and any kit you require. Work your body as hard as you can during your activities – no standing around on the tennis court or gentle pottering round the swimming pool!

Notes on particular activities are given at the end of this chapter and in Appendix B.

Every week: your basic fat-burning activity is walking.
Take a brisk walk every day. Aim to cover a *minimum* of 2 miles within half an hour. You can walk at any time of day but you will maximise fat-burning by going out within an hour after your main meal. If you want to take two or more 2-mile walks on any day, go ahead – it will speed up your progress.

Breathing exercises
Do these at least once a day. Breathing exercises before an activity session will speed up your body's response (see page 167).

Activity for muscle-building and to raise metabolic rate
The Fast Track requires as much activity as you can manage. The intention is to increase the power of the muscles in every part of your body. By putting regular demand on your muscles, you will increase the size and effectiveness of the mitochondria in every cell so that your capacity for burning food and fat to maintain a high metabolic rate is substantially increased. Extended periods of less intense activity will improve the enzyme systems which determine the body's ability to release fat from storage depots.

Always warm up before exercise and stretch out afterwards. Whenever possible, make your exercise session last a minimum of half an hour, increasing the length of time as your level of fitness increases. The longer you can make your exercise session last, the higher the proportion of fat burnt in order to fuel your activity, so do more while it feels good. Stop exercising or change to another activity when what you're doing becomes onerous – remember the pleasure principle! There is no point in gritting your teeth and struggling to continue with the same form of exercise when your muscles hurt or you are out of breath; this will only interfere with fat-burning and put you off activity. If you do overdo it so you are stiff next day, cut back next time. Give yourself a rest day when you do nothing more strenuous than walking as often as you feel you need it.

We have designed sample exercise schedules which allow one set of muscles to recover from a day's activity while you use other parts of your body. You can work out your own schedule from the table below if you wish. On any day, select your main activity from one of the three groups, using activities from one of the others next day and from the third on the third day.

Fast Track Activity Table

GROUP A	GROUP B	GROUP C
Running	Weight-training	Dancing
Cycling	Floor exercises	Swimming
Skipping	Digging	Rowing
Football	Heavy outdoor labour	Judo
Tennis (singles)		Karate
Badminton (singles)		
Squash		
Skiing		

For example, you could build your personal routine on a basis of a walk lasting a minimum of half an hour each day, on top of which you add more strenuous activity for another half hour on 5 days of the week. On Monday, you might go cycling (Group A). On Tuesday you could concentrate on Group B, with floor exercises, weight-training and press-ups (see Notes 3 and 6 at the end of this chapter). On Wednesday you might do nothing more strenuous than walking, and on Thursday return to Group A with a half-hour run. On Friday you could dance (Group C), and on Saturday go to a gym for a session of weight-training (Group B). Take a long walk on Sunday and repeat the sequence starting with a cycle ride on Monday. We give a more detailed description of this sort of schedule below but you should feel free to design one that is right for you.

After the first week or two, you will find you can exercise for longer and if you are determined to lose fat quickly, you will take every opportunity to do as much as you can. But always work within your capacity.

Never push yourself so hard that your muscles stay sore for more than one day and *never* take strenuous exercise when you are feeling ill or exhausted. If you heed these warnings, you will be able to continue on the Fast Track for as long as you wish. However, if you exercise too hard when you are not sufficiently fit, you are liable to make yourself ill and undermine your ability to deal with fat.

Rest completely at the first sign of infection such as a cold. If you become unwell, go to bed and get more sleep. Eat more fresh fruit and zinc-rich foods such as lean red meat, nuts, eggs, organic wholewheat and oats.

Fast Track Sample Schedule

WEEK 1

MONDAY
Breathing exercises (Appendix B, page 167) and 2-mile brisk walk.
Warm-up (Schedule C, page 181); dance (Note 2, page 126) or swim.
Repeat walk if desired.

TUESDAY
Breathing exercises and 2-mile walk.
Warm-up; floor exercises (Schedule C, page 181).

WEDNESDAY
Breathing exercises and 3-mile walk.

THURSDAY
Breathing exercises and 2-mile walk.
Warm-up; 20-minute run (Note 4, page 127) or 40 minutes' tennis, badminton or squash.

FRIDAY
Breathing exercises and 3-mile walk.

SATURDAY
Breathing exercises and 2-mile walk.
Warm-up; dance, row or swim.

SUNDAY
Breathing exercises.
Long walk (Note 5, page 128) or long cycle ride.

WEEK 2

MONDAY
Breathing exercises and 2-mile walk.
Warm-up; floor exercises.

TUESDAY
Breathing exercises and 2-mile walk.
Dance or swim.

WEDNESDAY
Breathing exercises and 3-mile walk.

THURSDAY
Breathing exercises and 2-mile walk.
Warm-up; 30-minute run or 1 hour's tennis, badminton or squash.

FRIDAY
Breathing exercises and 2-mile walk.
Warm-up; floor exercises, gym or weight-training (Note 3, page 126).

SATURDAY
Breathing exercises and 2-mile walk.
Dance, row or swim.

SUNDAY
Breathing exercises.
Long walk or long cycle ride.

WEEK 3 onwards

Your walk should now average 3 brisk miles every day. Alternate 2-mile and 4-mile days if you prefer.

Daily activity schedules continue as Week 2 but you will progress to longer exercise sessions, faster activities, heavier weights, more demanding games. The more you do, the more fat you'll burn but watch for signs of overdoing it.

2. Happy Medium Action Plan

Happy Medium Diet
Your first priority is to learn to be sensitive to your food

needs and to concentrate on meeting them. Eat little and often, snacking on complex carbohydrate foods such as vegetables, potatoes, organic rice cakes and unsweetened cereals with low-fat natural yoghurt or skimmed milk. Other suggestions follow:

1. Bread: if you like bread, eat it as often as you wish – but be careful about what you put on it. Any fat (butter, margarine, etc) should be spread as thinly as possible or avoided completely. Do not use sweet spreads such as honey or jam. Slice cheese thinly if you use it for sandwich fillings, combine with tomato or cucumber to add moistness and flavour.

2. Ensure high micronutrient intake. Eat nuts and seeds (2 or 3 ounces) and/or fresh fish (6 ounces) every day for minerals and essential fatty acids. Fish canned in brine is a reasonable substitute for fresh fish. Avoid frozen breaded or battered fish, and fish sold in sauce or with butter.

3. Maximise fat burning by eating your main protein meal of the day 2 or 3 hours before a session of demanding exercise. However, if you take less demanding exercise (your daily walk or cycle ride) within an hour of finishing a meal, it will be maximally effective. Stick to complex carbohydrates for supper, avoiding high-fat foods such as cheese and meat.

4. Take care to avoid processed or sweetened foods.

5. Avoid fried food. If you do fry, use very little oil. Cooking in a small quantity of stock using a heavy pan is better for your health and figure.

6. Incorrigible calorie counters should aim for about 2,000 daily (men: 2,500) in the first week, progressing to 2,300 to 2,800 (men: 2,800 to 3,400) by Week 4. People below average height and people over fifty may want a little less; taller, younger, or more muscular people may want more. Try to be sensitive to your own requirements: eat as much as

you want to avoid hunger, but don't eat when you don't need food. *All your food should be unprocessed and rich in nutrients.* (See menu suggestions, pages 162–66.)

Happy Medium Activity Schedule

Preparation
Make a list of your preferred activities and equip yourself with the right clothing, partners, venues and any kit you require. To raise your metabolic rate, you will need to work at your chosen activities – no standing around on the tennis court or gentle pottering round the swimming pool!

If you are under medical supervision for any condition, check with your doctor before embarking on this activity schedule. Your best health safeguard is to be especially attentive to feedback from your body when you exercise; when activity makes you feel bad, stop doing it. If you need medication which can increase exercise tolerance (eg pain-killers of any sort), you should consider changing to the Long Haul Track. *Never* take medicine to reduce pain before an exercise session: it is dangerous to block messages from your body.

Notes on particular activities are given at the end of this chapter and in Appendix B.

Every week: your basic fat-burning activity is walking
Take a walk every day. Go as far as you can, as often and as briskly as possible; you will burn more fat on one long walk than several shorter ones. Aim to cover a minimum of 2 miles within half an hour. You can walk at any time of day but you will maximise fat-burning by going out within an hour after your main meal. Always wear suitable shoes for walking; well-fitting trainers from a sports shop are ideal for roads and dry paths. If you are accustomed to walking, go faster than you normally would; focus your mind on a quick march (singing a jaunty song in your mind can be very helpful)

and take long strides, swinging your legs from the hips.

If you have problems with walking you may prefer 20 to 40 minutes' cycling, on a stationary bicycle if desired. Increase the length of your cycling sessions as your stamina improves.

Breathing Exercises
Do these at least once a day. Breathing exercises before an activity session will speed up your body's response. (See Appendix B, page 167.)

Activity to raise metabolic rate
Use a variety of types of exercise to increase the power of different muscle groups and reproportion your body while you burn off excess fat. The table below divides exercises into three groups; maximise the effectiveness of your activities by choosing exercises from different groups on successive exercise days.

Try to make each exercise session last at least half an hour; the longer you continue to exercise, the higher the proportion of fat used as fuel. Stop exercising or change to a different activity when what you are doing becomes onerous – remember the pleasure principle! If you overdo it so that you are stiff next day, reduce the length or intensity of your exercise session. Have three or four exercise days each week, alternating these with rest days when you do nothing more strenuous than walking and breathing exercises.

Happy Medium Activity Table

GROUP A	GROUP B	GROUP C
Jogging or running	Gym training	Aerobics
Tennis (singles)	EYT floor exercises	Swimming
Badminton (singles)	Heavy gardening (digging, hoeing)	Dancing
Cycling	Fencing	T'ai Chi

If you wish, you can create your own exercise schedule to match your preferences and fitness level but remember to take your daily walk and breathing exercises, whatever else you do. You might choose to do a Group A activity such as cycling on Monday, go to your local gym (Group B) on Wednesday, go swimming (Group C) on Friday, and take a really long walk – as far as you can go – on Sunday.

After the first couple of weeks, you will find you can exercise for longer, and if you are determined to shed fat as quickly as possible, you will take every opportunity for activity. But always work within your capacity. Avoid pushing yourself so hard that your muscles stay sore and *never* take strenuous exercise when you are feeling ill or exhausted.

Rest completely at the first sign of infection such as a cold. If you become unwell, go to bed and get more sleep. Eat more fresh fruit and zinc-rich foods such as lean red meat, nuts, eggs, organic wholewheat and oats.

Happy Medium Sample Schedule

WEEK 1

MONDAY
Breathing exercises and 2-mile brisk walk.
Warm-up (Schedule C, page 181); 20 minutes' dance (Note 2, page 126) or swim.

TUESDAY
Breathing exercises and 2-mile walk.

WEDNESDAY
Breathing exercises and 2-mile walk.
Warm-up; 10 minutes' floor exercises (Appendix B, page 170), 10-minute run (Note 4, page 127); *or* 30 minutes' tennis or badminton.

THURSDAY
Breathing exercises and 3-mile walk.

FRIDAY
Breathing exercises and 2-mile walk.
Warm-up; gym training (Note 3, page 126).

SATURDAY
Breathing exercises and 2-mile walk.
Warm-up; 20 minutes' dance.

SUNDAY
Breathing exercises.
Long walk (Note 5, page 128) or long cycle ride.

WEEK 2

MONDAY
Breathing exercises and 2-mile walk.
Warm-up; gym training or floor exercises.

TUESDAY
Breathing exercises and 3-mile walk.

WEDNESDAY
Breathing exercises and 2-mile walk.
Warm-up; 15-minute run *or* 40 minutes' tennis or bad-
minton.

THURSDAY
Breathing exercises and 3-mile walk.

FRIDAY
Breathing exercises and 2-mile walk.
15-minute swim.

SATURDAY
Breathing exercises and 3-mile walk.

SUNDAY
Breathing exercises.
Long walk or long cycle ride.

WEEK 3

MONDAY
Breathing exercise, and 2-mile walk.
Warm-up; gym training or floor exercises.

TUESDAY
Breathing exercises and 4-mile walk.

WEDNESDAY
Breathing exercises and 2-mile walk.
Warm-up; 20-minute run *or* 45 minutes' tennis or bad-minton.

THURSDAY
Breathing exercises and 4-mile walk.

FRIDAY
Breathing exercises and 2-mile walk.
15-minute swim.

SATURDAY
Breathing exercises and 2-mile walk.
Warm-up; 20 minutes' dance.

SUNDAY
Breathing exercises.
Long walk or long cycle ride.

WEEK 4 onwards

Your walk should now average 3 brisk miles a day.
Walk longer and further whenever you have time. Make
a habit of walking or cycling to shops, station or work.
  Daily activity schedules continue as Week 3 but you
will progress to longer exercise sessions and more
demanding games. The more you do, the more fat you'll
burn – but do not push yourself when you feel unwell
or uncomfortable.

3. Long Haul Action Plan

Long Haul Diet
Achieving the right balance between food and activity
is especially important on the Long Haul because it does
not put heavy demand on your body. Judge your needs
carefully by tuning into your appetite; eat whenever you
feel you need it and remember not to go hungry. As you

increase your activity level, you may find that your appetite diminishes. If this happens, do continue to make sure that you eat enough to satisfy your nutrient needs. This means taking in at least 2,000 calories in nutrient-rich food. See Menu 2, page 164 for an example of the sort of balanced diet that will deliver the nutrients you need every day.

This is a high-energy system and you must not be nervous about eating well. We do not wish to emphasise calorie-counts but we recognise that people who have had long-standing worries about the accumulation of fat will have become accustomed to counting calories and may shy away from nourishing foods such as nuts and seeds because of their high calorie content. We quote figures only to remind you that a more restricted diet will not help you to EAT YOURSELF THIN.

As you progress on the Long Haul, you will be training your body to use more food and burn off fat. Trust your body! Ignoring or overriding your inbuilt needs for adequate food and activity has failed you; now you are changing to succeed.

Long Haul Activity Schedule

Warning: If you have been directed to the Long Haul, it is because you are not sufficiently fit to cope safely with a heavy schedule of demanding activity. Discover your personal exercise capacity by increasing the length and intensity of activity sessions slowly and cautiously. It is especially important for you to work within your limits; *never* push yourself so hard that you feel stiff or sore for more than one day. Give your body plenty of time to become accustomed to exercise; patience early on will allow you to make more effective progress later.

If you are under medical supervision for any condition, you would be wise to check with your doctor before embarking on this activity schedule. The demands of the Long Haul are not likely to cause any damage *so long as you remain alert to feedback from your body*. When activity makes you feel bad, stop doing it. *Do not* push yourself so hard that you experience significant pain in any part of your body. Chest pain should be taken particularly seriously; if it happens, stop and rest. Try again later, do not give up exercise (it will improve your cardio-vascular health) but take it very gently so that you remain below the pain threshold.

If you regularly use any medication which can increase exercise tolerance (eg pain-killers, medicines for angina), you must be especially cautious. If you feel breathless, rest and start practising breathing exercises (page 167). *Never* take medicine to reduce pain before an exercise session: it is dangerous to block messages from your body.

Preparation
Make a list of your preferred activities (see table below for suggestions) and equip yourself with the right clothing, partners, venues and any kit you require.

Notes on particular activities are given at the end of this chapter and in Appendix B.

Every week: your basic fat-burning activity is walking

STAGE 1

EVERY DAY
Do breathing exercises (Appendix B) and go for a 15-minute walk. If possible, take two or more walks in a day. Walk whenever you feel most comfortable but be sure you are wearing suitable shoes such as well-fitting trainers from a sports shop. Walk briskly, but avoid going so fast that you suffer leg or chest pain. Breathe deeply, hold your head high and take fairly long strides, swinging your legs from the hip.

If walking causes problems, cycling is an acceptable substitute. Get a stationary bicycle if you prefer to exercise at home and use it for 15 minutes a day, or as long as your walk would last, progressively increasing the time and resistance. An indoor exercise

bicycle is particularly useful for those such as asth-
matics who have problems with winter exercise outdoors.

Continue with Stage 1 until a *regular* daily walk without
rests, lasting a minimum of 15 minutes, is well within
your capacity, then move on to Stage 2.

STAGE 2

EVERY DAY
Breathing exercises (Appendix B) and a half-hour
walk.

ALTERNATE DAYS
Floor exercises, Schedule A.

Continue Stage 2 for 2 weeks, or until you can walk 2
miles in half an hour or less every day.

STAGE 3

EVERY DAY
Breathing exercises and at least one 2-mile walk.

ALTERNATE DAYS
Floor exercises, Schedule B.

When Stage 3 activities present no challenge, take a
4-mile brisk walk. If you can cover this distance in an
hour, you are ready for Stage 4.

STAGE 4

You should now begin a wider range of activities.
While walking (or cycling) is your daily priority, the
Long Haul offers a variety of other activities that make
different demands on the body. We have divided them
into two groups (see table below). Choose activities
from each group on alternate exercise days to minimise muscle soreness and strain. Plan one exercise
session involving an activity from this list every two

days, but do not worry about missing a day if you are not feeling at your best.

The longer each exercise session lasts, the greater its effect will be, but you will have to get your body accustomed to activity before you attempt extended periods of exercise. Because of the importance of keeping within your personal limits, we cannot fix the length of time of any activity session. However, the general rules are simple: do as much as you can and carry on for as long as you can without straining yourself. It is much better to build up slowly than to move too fast and damage yourself.

If you are very over-fat, you may find that activities involving running or jogging cause joint pain. Change over to forms of activity where your weight is supported such as cycling or swimming until some of that fat has gone and your muscles are stronger.

Long Haul Activity Table

GROUP A	GROUP B
Jogging	Floor exercises
Cycling	Gym training
Swimming	Yoga
Dance	Gardening, outdoor labour
Badminton	
Tennis	

Long Haul Sample Schedule

STAGE 4, WEEK 1

MONDAY
Breathing exercises; half-hour walk.
Warm-up (page 181); floor exercises (Appendix B, page 170) or yoga.

TUESDAY
Breathing exercises; half-hour walk.

WEDNESDAY
Breathing exercises; half-hour walk.
Warm-up; dance (Note 2, page 126).

THURSDAY
Breathing exercises; half-hour walk.

FRIDAY
Breathing exercises; half-hour walk.
Warm-up; gym training (Note 3, page 126).

SATURDAY
Breathing exercises; half-hour walk.

SUNDAY
Breathing exercises; long walk (Note 5, page 128).

WEEK 2

MONDAY
Breathing exercises; half-hour walk.
Warm-up; floor exercises or gym training.

TUESDAY
Breathing exercises; 45-minute walk.

WEDNESDAY
Breathing exercises; half-hour walk.
Swim.

THURSDAY
Breathing exercises; 45-minute walk.

FRIDAY
Breathing exercises; half-hour walk.
Warm-up; gym training or yoga.

SATURDAY
Breathing exercises; 45-minute walk.

SUNDAY
Breathing exercises; long walk.

WEEK 3

MONDAY
Breathing exercises; half-hour walk.
Warm-up; floor exercises or gym training.

TUESDAY
Breathing exercises; one-hour walk.

WEDNESDAY
Breathing exercises; half-hour walk.
Swim.

THURSDAY
Breathing exercises; one-hour walk.

FRIDAY
Breathing exercises; half-hour walk.
Warm-up; dance or yoga.

SATURDAY
Breathing exercises; one-hour walk.

SUNDAY
Breathing exercises; long walk.

WEEK 4 and subsequent weeks

You are now quite accustomed to regular exercise! Carry on walking every day, adding in as many varied sessions of vigorous activity as you can. Extend the length of time as you become fitter. Follow your inclination into pleasurable activities and watch your body changing shape as it responds.

Notes on Activities

1. Warm-Up
You must warm up before any strenuous activity to get your systems ready to meet the demands you will make on them. Use Schedule C exercises from Appendix B,

page 171, before any such activity. If anything delays the start of your activity and you cool down, warm up again.

2. Dance

Dance is movement to music. It can be anything you wish to make it, from the individual's relaxed sensuality to the formality of formation events. Even disabled people can move parts of their bodies rhythmically to music for exercise and recreation. Suit your dance to your mood and your needs; these may change as you get into moving; go with it as far as you like. Those who are carrying a lot of fat can use dance as a way of building up capacity for activity, while at the same time getting in touch with their selves. Collect music that makes you want to move and use it frequently.

3. Gym training

There are many sorts of gyms around the country. If there is more than one in your area check them all out. Things to look for: enough basic equipment; racks of bar- and dumb-bells are a good sign because you will not spend time changing weights. Complicated machines should be treated with suspicion unless there are clear instructions that you can understand and you can set the machine up to do what you want. Is there always a competent person on hand, with whom you can discuss your precise needs? Do not be sold a standard course they happen to have. Are there good changing facilities; can you shower or sauna? Will you have all the time you need? Lastly, what will it cost? Pay as you go until you know how much you will need, do not join for life or commit yourself to a months-ahead payment schedule.

Local authority facilities are usually cheapest, but there may be a waiting list. If we were beginners, we would look for a local sports centre with competent staff, a positive atmosphere, and plenty of simple equipment. You can move on once you have found your feet.

Make sure you can follow your routine with the minimum of disruption; if you want to chat and socialise, do it in the shower or sauna after you have had your work-out.

Make sure that someone goes through your routine with you on your first session and shows you how to use the equipment safely. If you are in doubt always ask, and when you are experienced help others if they need it.

4. Running/jogging

If you have never done either of these, it is important to get the basics right. We are amazed at the number of seasoned joggers and runners we meet who just cannot move properly. While there are variations in style, many seem to have acquired peculiar shuffles or ungainly hops. Watch athletics on TV, see how, even when warming up, athletes move smoothly, rhythmically and easily. Notice the balancing swing of the arms, the long economical strides, the straight spine, the slight forward lean. Try to copy someone who looks right to you. If you have any difficulty, consult other runners or join an athletics club. Getting your style right at the beginning will be a sound investment for the future.

Get the right gear; good trainers, cotton socks, vest and shorts, and a track suit. Forget fashion and go for function; your local sports shop should be helpful.

Always warm up, even before the shortest run; see above. When you are warm and ready, head outdoors, try to stick to level ground away from traffic. Hard surfaces are better than slippery grass. Be prepared to go out in all except the most extreme weather.

Getting started. Taking long strides, walk at the fastest pace you can maintain for 5 minutes, then break into an easy trot until you begin to feel the strain, then walk for another 5 minutes. Repeat this sequence for 30 minutes. If you become breathless or your muscles ache continually, slow right down until you recover. Do not push yourself too hard until you understand what you are capable of doing. Build up the amount of time you spend trotting until you can continue for 20 minutes. Then start to vary your speed and length of stride. A good routine for general fitness is to mix brisk walking, trotting or jogging, with brief periods of fast running.

If you are a lapsed runner, do half of what you think you are capable of. Muscles can be re-trained quite quickly, but the longer you have been off, the longer your legs will take to return to competence. Mix walking and running if your legs give out first. Do not try to run through pain barriers, especially if your legs ache; this is lactate build-up and it will inhibit fat burning if you continue.

5. *Long walks*
Comfortable shoes or boots are essential. Blistered feet or pinched toes do not aid fat loss. You should also equip yourself to cope with the vagaries of the weather. Get a small knapsack that will hold all you need and make a day of it. You will find many others doing the same thing if you want to head for the popular walks, or you can go into the deep countryside and try some of the less used paths.

Maps and guides are readily available; become an explorer of the world around you. Remember the pleasure principle and do not grind past beauty spots or things which interest you; your metabolism will be burning away while you take time to stand and stare.

6. *Cycling*
You can substitute cycling for walking (or for using the car). It is not quite as good as walking for burning fat because it does not use the major muscle groups as effectively. Nevertheless it is a very enjoyable way of getting around.

A bicycle is a very efficient and subtle machine. If you have been used to a heavy, ill-adjusted hulk you might be amazed at the difference a modern lightweight can make to your ideas of cycling. You may be able to hire one for a trial; make sure you can adjust seat and handlebars so that it feels right for you, and do not be afraid to experiment. Get a proper racing saddle for long-term comfort; a soft, wide saddle will make you sore, whereas you will hardly notice the support of a good saddle. A 'Ladies' Madison' is particularly good for women.

7. Re-proportioning

Weight-training is the most efficient method of re-proportioning your body. See the general advice in the previous chapter. Do not go straight for a course of specific exercises if you have not previously used weight-training. Acclimatise with a general fitness routine over a period of weeks; after this you may find that you need not worry, or that what you need is different from what you had thought. Once you are sure, seek specific help either from a qualified instructor or from specialised publications.

Action Now

○ *Once you know which Action Plan is for you, persevere with it. The long-term benefits will pay off permanently!*

CHAPTER 10

Final Phase – Balance

THE FINAL OBJECTIVE of your new lifestyle is to achieve a state where being slim is automatic. This occurs when all the factors affecting the proportion of fat you carry are in balance at a level *you* choose.

The concept of balance is easy to grasp. Ordinarily it is a static state, but in living systems it is dynamic because things are changing all the time. The best picture for balance in life is not of scales, but of a juggler keeping everything in perfect motion. Balance can happen at many levels. Thus the fat person is one sort of balance, with a low metabolic rate balanced by low food input and low energy availability. The balance you are aiming for is based on a high metabolic rate, where food and energy are in constant flow through your body.

Balance is easier to maintain with a high metabolic rate because it takes more to throw it off. The dieter is susceptible to the effects of the smallest cream cake; with a high metabolic rate you will be able to eat them and hardly notice. To a low metabolism a cream cake can be a fattening mountain; to a high metabolism it is just a tasty morsel.

The ideal is to live in a way which makes balance itself automatic. Many body systems do this by a process called *homeostasis*. The best known example is body temperature, which remains constant except under extreme circumstances; insulin surging as the body attempts to maintain constant blood sugar levels is another instance. Balance ceases to be automatic when we have choice and do not understand the effects of the actions we take, as in the food we eat or the way we choose to live. EAT YOURSELF THIN has aimed at teaching you how to live so that your body does not need fat –

at creating the dynamic balance of a thin person.

Because life changes and the centre of balance shifts, this book can only explain the means of achieving balance; you will have to learn how to do it. You can do this much as circus performers do. Although they may be a long way up, on a very thin wire and carrying a heavy pole, they actually balance by applying a few established rules and some minor adjustments. In this way the whole task is made as easy as possible; if it were impossibly difficult they would not do it night after night.

The same applies to achieving balance in your life. You have the established rules: eating enough of the right food; getting enough oxygen into your system, and being sufficiently active to use the energy you are producing. Minor adjustments to these factors should help you keep in balance as life and circumstances change around you.

Like the tightrope walker, you can use things which might be seen as disruptors to actually help you. Our old enemy hunger is the prime example. We have seen how, by clinging to it through thick and thin, dieters get fat. You, on the other hand, have experienced a lack of hunger which energises and stimulates you and allows unwanted fat to be shed. That does not mean hunger has no part to play in your life; it does, but only as a minor means of adjustment to maintain balance.

In eating the sorts of food we recommend you will find out about your personal nutritional needs. It is important that you get the full range of micronutrients. Although we have given general advice, only you can do the fine tuning in relation to your own needs and experience. Individual variability must never be overlooked, nor must the variations which occur within the lives of individuals. When you have achieved control over your changing needs you will be a master of your art, the art which created the new you. There is no short cut; such discoveries are part of the joy of life and a much better use of your talents than meaningless calorie counting.

Tune in to yourself and your body will lead you towards what is good for you; in this way it will help you make the right choices and maintain nutritional balance. The balance you create will spread beyond the immediate effects of remaining thin. Many experts believe that much of the ill health we suffer can be avoided by proper nutritional balance and your experience is likely to bear this out.

The positive use of hunger involves *just* avoiding it. In Chapter Seven we explained that you must keep enough food energy in circulation to meet all your needs. Too little, and your body will lower its metabolic rate to conserve energy as fat.

You should always aim to eat enough so that, whatever your circumstances, you have a little more than you need. Ideally, if you were to leave one tenth of your food, you would feel hungry. Since you should not feel hungry on principle, eating the right amount to maintain this balance is, frankly, tricky. You will only come to it through listening to your body and knowing its needs.

If your shape is stable and satisfactory you can assume you are eating enough to meet your needs. One way to learn how far ahead of hunger you are is to drop back a little. Eat slightly less on consecutive similar days, and you will find out if you feel hungry. If so fine, you have got the balance about right, put your food intake back to its former level and carry on. If not, hold the reduced input for another day and see what happens. If after 3 days you do not feel hungry, and good flesh is not melting from your bones, you could cut back another 10%. But if your shape is stable, why bother? You do not need to provoke effects when things are going fine.

Do not test yourself if things are going well. And when you do, be aware of the slightest twinge of hunger – and eradicate it. Beware of slipping into obsession with the old enemy; it is better forgotten; you have much more interesting things to occupy your time.

Do remember that outside factors will tend to unbalance you. Emotions, hormone cycles, unexpected physical demands, infections and the weather all affect your use of food. Listen to and trust your body; you should have a very good working relationship by now. If you must err, do so on the side of eating too much. Your body is likely to maintain a healthy balance and just burn off anything not needed. Serious excess can always be lost later, but you cannot make up for deficiencies of things your body needed at the time.

Now you know how to EAT YOURSELF THIN, shedding a little fat is no problem should you over-eat occasionally. This means you need not fear the good times. No more sparrow pecks at Christmas or other celebrations; enjoy yourself with complete confidence that you can burn it off next week and not show the difference.

You can use breathing as a positive help to maintain balance. Those demands in life which tend to centre around other people, varying from the mildly irritating to the frankly infuriating, can throw your emotions and hormones off balance. These episodes may cause eddies through your metabolism for days unless they are neutralised. There are two ways of dealing with these situations; either you give full and loud vent to your true feelings, or you absorb and contain the reaction as harmlessly as you can. Whenever possible, without destroying your relationship or career, go for the former! Realistically, we know this is seldom an option, so you must limit the reaction within yourself before it gets out of hand. Deep breathing, with activity if possible, to use the energy produced by adrenalin, is the best answer. Get excessive oxygen flowing around your body and you will be able to ride above, rather than get involved in, the storm around you.

If you can anticipate a sticky patch and prepare beforehand by oxygenating, you will be at an advantage. You may even prevent the expected situation simply by your calm presence! Control of your self will inevitably extend outwards and give you more control over your interactions with others.

The most obvious change in your transition to a thin person is in the amount of activity you are doing. This must be balanced by adequate rest, relaxation and good sound sleep. You may find that you are sleeping better and longer as a result of your increased activity. This is a very good thing because when you are asleep your brain changes its priorities, away from action and movement to repair and rebuild. Increasing your metabolic rate means that in addition to putting out more energy, you will also need more repair and maintenance. This will help you renew and rejuvenate, not only keeping your body working well but looking good as well; bright eyes, a glowing skin and shining hair are indicators of a healthy metabolism. These things are produced during sound sleep.

We should have a balanced perspective of exercise. Although we have combined exercise with eating enough of the right food and oxygenating your body to produce a thin way of life, the last two are very natural things. Exercise, in the formal and ordered way most of us do it, is not. It is a substitute for a way of life which in itself is out of balance. The amount of emphasis we have given to this aspect of a slim person's way of life reflects this.

In the Western industrial world most of us lead lives from which natural activity has largely been removed and we have to devise ways to put it back. This has advantages; you can choose to do enjoyable things in place of drudgery. But there are disadvantages; you have consciously to build activity into your life and maintain your motivation to pursue it. Understanding the need for activity to balance the advantages of modern life should help with motivation.

Physical activity is also the key to maintaining balance at many levels. Once you have become accustomed to an active way of life you will find you miss it during periods of enforced inactivity. Your body will be softly nagging you to do what it needs. Adjusting your activity on a week by week basis is the only way to keep your body in the sort of shape you want. As with food, there will come a time when you will wish to ease off a little and see what happens. If you keep eating the same amount, you may put on a little fat. You can either increase your activity rate and burn it, or drop your food intake (*not* to the point where you are hungry) and watch it melt away.

Your activity level will also affect your hormone profile. Many women are surprised that just walking for half an hour a day can have beneficial effects on troublesome aspects of their monthly cycle. You will be amazed how adaptable your body can be. It is up to you to use this adaptability in the way that suits you best. Experience will guide you to the activity/hormone balance that is most appropriate. And once you have learned how to modify your hormone profile, you can adjust it as time and circumstances change your needs.

Minor aches and pains can also be helpful signals. There will be times when you are being physical when the energy just will not turn on. You may get a pain in your chest, on the right-hand side just under your ribs, instead of the smooth energy flow you are expecting. The most likely cause is your liver; instead of turning on its glycogen stores, it is saying it is preoccupied and would rather not do so. You have to decide how far to push it. If the cause is night-before excesses, it may be OK to push on, but if it is dealing with an infection or hormone excesses, you would do better to listen to your body and give it a miss. See what happens tomorrow.

Similarly, muscular aches and stiffness without obvious cause can be a forewarning of an infection. Aches and that lack-lustre, under-the-weather feeling can be caused by interferons fighting off an infection. If you let them do their job, you are unlikely to go down with it. If you insist on using energy for activity, you may help the infection get hold. It is far better to take early avoiding action, resting, keeping warm and drinking plenty of fresh fruit juice, than to suffer unnecessary and perhaps extended illness.

When you are following your activity programme you will experience a physical limit. This may be breathlessness, where you cannot get enough oxygen in for the energy output you require; more likely you will find that one group of muscles or joints is not as strong as the rest of your body. It will let you know by persistently being the first to ache or refuse to function. This is an important message which tells you of an imbalance in your physiology. The answer is to give that part special care and attention; more work within your capacity to build it up, more pampering, such as massage, to aid recovery. This extra care will be rewarded when your body comes into balance and you are capable of much more because you have no weak points that let you down.

You will also find that activity can alter your moods. At those times of depression which hit us all occasionally, getting on your bike or putting on your running shoes and shaking up the brain chemistry can work wonders. The changes in general body chemistry brought about by activity will also affect other areas of your behaviour. You will find that your appetite in many areas will have grown.

This should not surprise you. In changing, you will have grown. You will have become more aware of your needs through eating the right foods; you will also have become aware of just how bad the average diet is. You will have become more physically competent, and more confident in the way you react to others and the world in general. And you will find that things you just did not believe to be possible were, in fact, within your grasp. Are you the same person who started reading this book?

As we have said already, you are an artist of your self, and changing your body is your greatest creative act. You should be aware of the effects this may have on those around you, because you may wish to change yourself, but at the same time keep your relationships in balance. The best answer to potential relationship problems is to take your friends and relatives with you. There is no reason why, in improving yourself, you should not spread the benefits to others.

The unattached young may find it a source of new friends with similar interests. Physical activities involving sports also have their social side. For mothers with young families, eating right and being more active can bring nothing but good to all the family. Recent research has convincingly associated improved intellectual performance among children with improved nutrition, and a family diet based on organic wholefoods is the most nutritious food you can get. Do not worry about children becoming fat on complex carbohydrates; what is true for you is true for them. Children have a naturally high metabolic rate, unless it is depressed by modern processed junk, and they will thrive on the same foods as you.

If your husband has grown used to you as a flabby, depressed person, he may be in for a shock. Whether it is a pleasant shock or otherwise depends on the nature of your relationship. There is no denying that many men like their women to be down; they are less demanding and threatening in that unnatural state. It is equally true that many women, although they go through the fat-loss motions, actually want to stay fat, hopeless and helplessly dependent. If you are serious about change, you must be aware that it could affect your relationship, and prepare accordingly. Take your man with you if you can; the lifestyle you are aiming for will protect him from heart disease, the main killer of males. If he won't go, you may have to leave him behind. Only you can judge whether your relationship can cope with that. Slow and subtle change may be the answer, or perhaps a full and frank discussion and agreed action.

Since most of this book has been written with a female bias, because excess fat tends to affect women more than men, we will direct the last words of this chapter to the men because we know many have fat problems and seek an effective answer. Everything we have said in EAT

YOURSELF THIN applies to men as much as women; where there are inapplicable passages they will be obvious. Men who set out to change their bodies and their selves run the same risks in their relationships as women.

By becoming a more physical animal you may be seen as intimidating; your changing food demands may create insecurities; the change in your priorities may disrupt accepted patterns within the family. Being aware that these things may happen will help to avoid any unexpected effects. The best solution for men is the same as for women: take your friends and relatives with you. The new balanced lifestyle you are both aiming for will be better for you both, for your relationship and your children.

Summary

- Being slim is automatic when all the factors affecting the proportion of fat on your body are in the right balance.
- The ideal is to live in a way which makes this balance automatic; your weight problem will be a thing of the past.
- When you understand how to balance food and activity, you are in control.

Action Now

- ○ *Take your family and friends with you into your new slim life!*

Troubles Surmounted

THE PUREST INTENTIONS and best laid plans can be disrupted when life takes an unexpected turn. Sometimes it will be impossible for you to keep to the plan you have selected. At other times, you may believe you are doing everything as you should, without getting the benefits that you expect. In this chapter, we explain how you can cope with a variety of problems that you may confront when trying to eat yourself thin.

Chapter Contents

1. Short-term disruption

One of the great advantages of EATING YOURSELF THIN is that you will not be significantly affected by short periods of poor diet or reduced activity levels. Naturally, you won't carry on shedding fat when you are not on track and if you deviate too far for too long you are likely to start putting fat on again; but that will not happen fast unless your eating patterns really go wildly haywire. Any fat you gain through reversion will come off quickly without extra effort once you're on course again.

This is the advantage of building a high metabolic rate: it allows your body to weather changes without going straight into fat-conservation mode. What you must do, as far as you possibly can, is maintain your metabolic rate at the highest possible level even when you are unable to stick to your EAT YOURSELF THIN Action Plan. This has two complications. First, you must try to keep your intake of complex carbohydrates high and not slip into anxious fat-person behaviour, refusing the potatoes and cereals lest you get fat again. Second, stay as physically active as you can.

2. When it's impossible to keep on-track

a: Diet
There are times when we cannot exert much control over what we get to eat. Travelling, business trips or holidays, conferences and courses, hospitalisation, crises at work or at home that take all your time ... any of these can disrupt your diet.

Regrettably, fast food and institutional catering almost always means unsatisfactory diet. Most organisations select foods for convenience and cheapness; nutritional value is low on their list of priorities. Such products can make you fat unless you make careful choices.

Cope as well as possible by avoiding sweetened and fatty foods. Select raw, fresh food – salads and fresh fruit. Take big helpings of the good stuff; do not be embarrassed. Cooked food should be as simple as possible, eg baked potatoes, grilled fish. Ask for yours without butter: most cooks pile on large quantities. Avoid fried foods. Refuse chips, biscuits, puddings. You may have to eat slightly less than usual, but don't starve yourself in your efforts to avoid unhealthy food. If necessary, supplement the diet provided with additional fresh fruit and nuts or other healthy snacks. Vegetarian menus are usually better for you. Look for wholefood restaurants if you're eating out.

Ironically, hospital menus are among the worst of all. If you have to stay in a hospital where healthy meals like salads are not normally provided, ask for the low-fat diet. If a reason is needed – beyond your simple desire for good health – you could say you have problems digesting fats, implying perhaps that you've had gall bladder trouble! Make your demands heard for basic wholefoods like wholemeal bread, whole rice. Hospitals, after all, are supposed to be concerned with health.

More healthy drinks are now available; most caterers offer natural mineral waters or unsweetened fruit juices. Ask for them if you can't see them on display. When disruption is due to parties or celebrations, enjoy them. They don't happen every day; eat and drink what you like! Your metabolic rate should be high enough to cope. If you're really trying to shed fat fast, you can always compensate with a longer exercise session next day – providing you are fit enough to cope with both excesses.

b: Activity
If it is impossible to keep to your normal activity schedule for any length of time, improvise as best you can. Take full advantage of any opportunities you find. If you're travelling, take exercise clothes and trainers with you. Most large hotels have swimming pools, sometimes gyms. Go for walks whenever possible, even if you are very busy. Activity will ease the stress of travel, refresh your mind and help you cope with a heavy workload.

When you are away on business, a walk outside or exercise session in your room before breakfast will wake your mind up ready for the day and help keep your metabolic rate high. After lunch or dinner, don't sit around chatting in a smoke-filled bar; take a brisk walk outdoors. Don't forget *your* need for physical activity just because your colleagues don't bother!

If you're on holiday, build activity into your daily schedule. Best of all, choose an activity holiday where you can learn new sports or return to activities you once enjoyed. There are growing numbers of such holidays offering a wide variety of activities you can try. It will be far more refreshing than lazing in the sun.

3. Illness

Illness usually means you've been under strain or your nutritional state is not yet good enough for high resistance. Have you been trying to shed fat too fast? Take illness as a warning that things could get worse unless you look after yourself better. It is vitally important that you rest when you feel ill. Take to your bed; sleep helps healing and there is no virtue in extending your illness by trying to continue as normal when your energy levels are low.

a. Infection

Eat more fresh fruit, especially citrus fruit and berries. Six oranges a day is not excessive if you're fighting a cold. The body uses vitamins faster when you have an infection.

Do not take strenuous exercise when you are unwell. Do nothing more strenuous than walking and deep breathing until you are fully fit, then ease yourself back with a less demanding regime for 2 weeks. For example, if you were on the Fast Track when you became ill, change to Happy Medium. Start at the beginning again; you can increase the pace when you are ready. Even a cold makes a heavy demand on your body and continuing with a demanding exercise schedule and rapid fat-burning will delay your recovery.

b. Injury

Never try to 'run through' an injury. Heed the message inherent in pain.

Most minor injuries should not be too disruptive but you must not let your enthusiasm lead you to stress the injured part. Healing requires rest initially then *gentle* activity until recovery is complete.

Injuries to the back, legs or feet that make walking difficult and running impossible will mean you have to take a break from your activity schedule. Reduce your food intake slightly to allow for reduced energy output – but do not go hungry. Keep your metabolic rate up by working uninjured parts. Perhaps this is the time to develop shapely shoulders and attractive back or pectoral muscles? Remember the wheelchair athletes and don't let your fitness decline if you can avoid it.

c. Getting back after time off

The key to getting fit again is to take things gently at first. Do not try to start where you left off. Be particularly careful after infection not to stress your body excessively; you could suffer a relapse. Warning signs that you're not ready for strenuous activity include tiredness, inability to warm up properly or an unusually high heart-rate that accelerates quickly. If you feel strange in any way, do not continue exercising; rest for a while, then take a walk if you wish. Try more strenuous activity again if you feel fine after another 2 or 3 days.

You will find out by experience how much you can do without excessive tiredness or discomfort; always respect your limits. If you were fit initially, you should find your strength comes back quite quickly, but you cannot expect your body to return to a trained state immediately.

Make sure you feed yourself well throughout the recovery period; do not try to cut back the calories for fear of putting your newly lost fat back on. On the EAT YOURSELF THIN system you will shed any excess fat faster and more easily when you return after a break. So just accept any slight increase in the amount of fat you're carrying; your body may need it to deal with your condition. It won't last long once you are fit again.

d. Recurrent illness

This means that something is awry in your life. Check your diet first; compare what you actually eat against the recommendations in Chapters Five and Six.

If your diet is good, the next most probable cause is emotional stress. Are there problems in your life that you have been unable to deal with? Try to stand back and assess your situation. If your emotional needs are not being met, see if you can develop a plan that will help you to get what you, personally, want. We are taught that unselfishness is a virtue; but when you put yourself and your own interests in second place too often, you will not be able to give of your best. A counsellor may be able to help.

Whatever the cause of recurrent illness, a heavy exercise schedule will make matters worse, while regular gentle activity will tend to help. Drop back to a less demanding track until your health improves.

e. Chronic illness

If you suffer from chronic illness, your condition is likely to improve when you embark on EATING YOURSELF THIN. The combination of plentiful good food and a gradually increasing activity level will aid recovery even from such serious diseases as diabetes, cancer and cardiovascular problems. However, it is imperative that chronically ill people attend closely to the feedback they get from their bodies.

Never take extra medication to prevent exercise-induced pain. If exercise can bring on pain, just do as much as you can as often as possible without setting the pain off. You may have to judge the level very carefully and it will vary from day to day. You can increase your pain-free exercise capacity but pushing yourself into pain could make your condition worse.

Consult your doctor before taking up any activity more strenuous than walking or cycling if you suffer from any serious illness.

f. Medication
Some medicines can induce weight gain. This is an acknowledged side-effect of many different types of drug, from anti-depressants to hormones; and some people find the fat they put on during a course of medication proves particularly difficult to shift. If you are in this situation, our book *Persistent Fat and How to Lose It* explains the reasons and how to cope.

The best way of dealing with this problem is to avoid using drugs whenever possible. Once you are well established on the EAT YOURSELF THIN system, you will be less vulnerable to illness of all kinds because your body's basic needs will be met. In general, you can anticipate that you will require less medication, and if you are using drugs on a regular basis now, you may be able to discontinue them. Discuss this possibility with your doctor and read our book *Alternatives to Drugs* for specific advice.

4. Excessive tiredness/aches/depression during or after exercise

Are you eating enough carbohydrate? Simple lack of adequate nourishment is the most common reason for problems with exercise. But if you're eating as much as we recommend in Chapters Six and Seven, you may be doing too much for your body to cope.

Often, activity has the paradoxical effect of relieving feelings of tiredness, especially when they're due to the stress of a sedentary occupation. But exercise will make tiredness worse when you are really exhausted. Try refreshing yet relatively undemanding exercise, like a brisk walk; mental and emotional exhaustion responds well to this and you will probably find it relaxes you so you sleep better.

Sometimes you will just experience a block that cuts off your access to energy. You may go out for a game of badminton and find you're collapsing halfway through. Or you may go for a run, only to find that your head begins to ache or you start to feel nauseated. These can be toxic reactions; your system may be preoccupied with coping with something that you may not even realise you encountered. They can occur after exposure to chemicals, such as solvents, to which you are sensitive. Do not go against such feelings; take things easy until they pass, trust your body to guide you. When accustomed effort produces unaccustomed ill-effects, the time is no longer right for effort.

Always heed warnings from your body; never try to override these messages. There are the people who run marathons when they're fighting viruses and collapse with overwhelming infections, or who, like the late Jim Fixx, insist on running through the pain of angina and push themselves to heart attacks. These people have too little respect for their bodies; they go for the mind-over-matter approach instead of aiming for understanding and internal consistency. There's no future in that.

5. Lack of progress

You believe you are on track but you do not seem to be burning off your excess fat. What could be going wrong?

First, how long have you been eating yourself thin? If you have only been on track for a few weeks, the results may not be showing up yet; your body could still be adjusting to your lifestyle changes. Give the system time to work! All your metabolic priorities and pathways may need to change and if you have had problems with excess fat for a long time, you will have to be patient. You have taken years to get where you are now; it may be some months before the effects of a metabolic turnaround in your body become obvious.

Apart from this, the most common reasons for lack of progress are cerebration, plateauing and incorrect timing. Read on to discover whether one of these applies to you.

a. Cerebration
Are you really as active as you think? Survey research, relying on reported exercise, suggests that virtually everyone takes regular exercise; but when researchers check what people actually do rather than asking what they *think* they do, they discover that active people are uncommon.

Keep a diary of your progress, noting how often you exercise, what you do, how long you continue, and the effects you experience. You may find that you imagine you do all we recommend, but in reality you miss too many exercise sessions, forget to walk every day, or devote too little time to activity. Also note all the occasions when you indulge in sweetened or processed food. You may be deviating too far from a nutritious diet to gain the benefits of EATING YOURSELF THIN.

b. Plateauing and timing
When you do roughly the same things every week, your body becomes accustomed to them. You achieve a stable balance between input and output that puts minimum stress on the body. This is the outcome that we have described in Chapter Ten. If your balance point comes before you have lost as much fat as you desire, you may not be satisfied with it and it may be necessary to increase your activity level or adjust your diet.

The plateau may, however, be a temporary feature of continuing change in your body. Change never occurs at a constant rate in living systems. Rapid change usually alternates with apparent stability in a stepwise sequence. At times you may despair when you are in a stable phase because your effort seems to achieve nothing; but suddenly, often for no apparent reason, things begin to change again and you enjoy the benefits of your perseverence. So if you are quite sure you are on track, just carry on: the results will become evident in due course. After all, a healthy lifestyle has no time limit!

If you want to induce faster change, you may be able to get off the plateau by increasing the time or intensity of exercise, or by taking up a new sport. You may have settled into a plodding routine to which you have adapted, but which makes too little demand on your metabolism to force your body to burn fat.

Plateaux can also develop when you fail to exercise for long enough to progress beyond the stage when your muscles are fuelled with glycogen, to the use of fat. Brief activity sessions may be insufficient to change your metabolic priorities so that you use up fat. Reducing the intensity of exercise to ensure that you can continue for 40 minutes or more at a time could solve your problem. Remember, the longer you continue exercising, the greater the proportion of fuel that comes from fat.

6. Food intolerance, sensitivity and addiction

Increasing numbers of people are suffering bad reactions to foods. Their immune systems become progressively overloaded with pollutants and synthetic chemicals. Eating organic food – particularly seeds, nuts and fish, all rich in essential fatty acids – will help to protect you from these problems.

a. Food intolerance and sensitivity

If you are sure that a particular food does not agree with you, then you should not eat it. However, recent concern about food allergy and related issues has led many people to restrict their diets quiet unnecessarily because they link illness with food without checking that their suspicions are correct. Many people erroneously come to believe that *all* forms of a certain class of food (eg nuts) will make them ill without realising that different varieties have different effects on the body. While peanuts, for example, may make you ill if you are sensitive to them, it is extremely unlikely that any other nuts will affect you the same way. So be cautious before you deem yourself allergic to any type of food.

Nevertheless, food intolerance is often linked with weight problems. If you suspect any particular food, leave it out of your diet *completely* for at least a week, then try it and look for any untoward symptoms. If you do get a bad reaction, you may want to repeat the process to check if the reaction was actually associated with the food and not just a coincidence. When you're sure you are intolerant to a food, test related foods to see whether your intolerance spreads to them. For example, some people are intolerant of wheat, oats and barley, while others, although sensitive to wheat, can digest oats with no difficulty. There is a comprehensive list of foods and the groups they belong to, as well as a detailed strategy for dealing with intolerance, in *Chemical Children* by Peter Mansfield and Jean Monroe (Century).

b. Food addiction

This is linked with intolerance. Paradoxically, addiction seems to be part of the body's way of coping with foods that produce bad reactions.

When you eat or drink any particular substance many times every day, you could be addicted. Can you imagine life without tea or coffee or toast? How do you feel when you run out of your daily favourites? If you never allow yourself to run out, you may be an addict.

While food addiction may sometimes be incon-sequential, it can cause a range of problems. First, it can maintain fat stores if the body reacts to the addictive substance as a toxin and your detoxification capacity is close to the point of overload. Second, it makes it imposs-ible for you to judge whether you actually need the food value that substance represents. If you are addicted to wheat, for example, you may eat a great deal of bread every day – whether you need it or not. Rather than meeting your body's needs, you are feeding your addic-tion. Third, the food to which you are addicted may cause intolerance symptoms ranging from emotional disturbance to colitis. Check out addiction problems in the same way as you check for food intolerance (*a, above*). If you are addicted, you'll crave the food or drink you're avoiding. You may suffer withdrawal symptoms. Headaches are common symptoms of coffee and tea withdrawal, but you may feel much better once the addictive substance is out of your system.

If you experience obvious symptoms of intolerance when you try the substance after a period of abstinence, you will probably decide to stop eating it. What you do will in any case depend on the severity of your reaction, but it is clearly wise to avoid food that produces definite unpleasant symptoms.

c. Sugar cravings

Craving for sweetness can be seen as a special case of food addiction. If you react badly to sugar, it will give you an instant lift followed by longer-lasting depression when you want more sugar. This pattern is associated with excessive insulin production, rapid fat deposition and problems with using fat for energy.

The only way to break out of this unhealthy cycle is to refuse sweet foods until your body becomes accustomed to coping without them. Reduce your desire for sweetness by making sure you get plenty of complex carbohydrates (page 60) before you become too hungry. Increase your intake of peas and beans to stabilise blood sugar.

Do not replace sugar with synthetic sweeteners – you will only perpetuate your problem. Artificial sweeteners produce an insulin reaction just like sugar, because your body associates a sweet taste with the need for insulin to clear sugar from the blood: the body's control systems evolved long before today's sweeteners were developed! A short time after you've had your sugar-free synthetically sweetened snack or drink, you'll feel hungry – much more hungry than you would have felt if you hadn't had it. What's more the extra insulin will already have shifted sugar from your blood into your fat cells.

So, artificial sweeteners, diet colas and the like may not contain many calories – but they can certainly make you fat. Give them up.

7. Fear of success

Do you foresee problems all the way with EATING YOUR-SELF THIN? Are you unable to keep to any healthy diet or continue with regular exercise? Do you slip straight back into fat, unhealthy ways of living after a few days or weeks of looking after yourself? If so, your problem could be fear of success – fear of confronting life without your protective layer of fat.

There are many interlinked psychological patterns which can produce the same effect. You may be afraid of taking responsibility for yourself, afraid to acknowledge that you are largely what you make of yourself. Women are brought up to be passive, allowing things to happen to them instead of exerting control over events: this is part of British culture.

To get slim and stay that way, you are going to have to take control over your life. Do you really want to let this opportunity slip away? Look into the future: think where the fat road leads and then look at a slim, healthy future. The only road that works for you – or anyone – is the positive one, the one that leads directly to your goal and beyond. Take it! You can do it! Do not underestimate yourself or your strength. Keep on telling yourself it's your life, your body, and you are going to make the very best of it. Why should you be content with anything less?

You may fear getting slim because it will expose you as an attractive, sexual creature who will have to start coping with advances from suitors. Fear of sex is often at the root of fat behaviour. Working through your emotional confusion with a counsellor from 'Relate' (the number is in the phone book; you may find it is under the previous name of 'Marriage Guidance') could free you from the bonds that were keeping you fat.

8. Emotional problems

Do you eat excessively when you're depressed, bored, angry, upset? If so, the answer is simple – just carry on with the EAT YOURSELF THIN system! Sometimes you'll eat more than you need but with your increased rate of metabolism, this won't cause you to pile on the fat in the way it used to. Match your eating with more activity, and you'll actually change your brain chemistry so that those destructive emotions don't cause damage. Physical activity lifts depression, calms anger, and makes you feel very much better.

That is not to say you should neglect the underlying problems which upset you; but life is not always peaceful and happy and we all have emotional ups and downs. Eating yourself thin will help to keep you on a more even keel.

9. Relationships and family problems

If your partner or family feel safer with you when you're fat, you will come under pressure to return to your fat lifestyle. Watch out for attempts to undermine your determination to eat the right types of food and become more active and don't take negative comments at face value. Such comments usually reflect the other person's problems. You must be careful not to take them on to your own back.

Your husband may fear – though perhaps not at a conscious level – that you will leave him for someone more exciting as soon as you become slim. Your children may see slim mothers as less cuddly if the picture they have of a proper mum developed when you were fat. So don't let them tease you or make you feel so foolish that you give up exercise; try to talk through their objections with them and help them understand why they may want you to stay fat when you want to be slim. Even if they're not entirely convinced, they won't carry on teasing when they find out how serious you are – especially if jibes lead to deep analytical discussion or ejection from the room!

Of course, you may decide that you won't get quite as thin as you'd planned if you find that your partner really doesn't like it. That's a perfectly reasonable decision so long as you are fit enough for long-term good health. Nobody has the right to expect you to be so fat you're unhealthy, but there's no harm in becoming your partner's fantasy object if you feel fine that way – but make sure it is your choice.

Changing yourself always affects your relationships. When you are moving towards a healthier, happier self, your old friends may start to feel inferior. They may not want to see you becoming self-determined, taking control of your life; it can disrupt old patterns and their comfortable assumptions about you.

What can you do? One possibility is that you will move on to a new group of relationships, new friends who are part of your new healthy lifestyle. As we change, we always leave some people behind and find others; those who stick with the same group all their lives tend to be the people who don't try to make anything of their lives. There's no going backwards and no sense in staying the same if it made you unhealthy and unhappy.

Of course, you can try to persuade your friends and family to join you. When they see how well you're looking, they will be convinced that the method works. With luck, they'll be willing to put in the necessary effort themselves and then you'll have company to share your newfound pleasure in good food and activity.

10. Energy drains, fears and inhibitions

You may believe in everything in EAT YOURSELF THIN, yet you feel you can't do it – can't change your diet, can't take more exercise, can't learn thin-person behaviour. We know from personal experience what it is to lack self-confidence, to have to work at belief before success is possible.

Are you undermined by self-doubt? Are you convinced that your problems are really laziness, greed and your inability to force yourself to change? If so, your first task is to work on your attitudes.

Whenever you set out to achieve something, you are more likely to reach your goal if your attitudes are positive. You must start with your sincere intention to become slim, attractive and healthy. Fix that goal firmly in your mind, focus on what you want to be, not on the reasons you could fail. Tell yourself you will enjoy using your body, not that you're a slow person who dislikes activity. You make success more probable by allowing yourself to believe it will happen. The potential for high-energy living is within you, you just have to tune in to it.

Keep your mind on the goal ahead of you, and your mental and spiritual energies will amplify your physical energy. Human beings need internal consistency. When activity and belief are directed the same way, you feel good and work well. But strive for activity when belief says you'll fail, and you will have to struggle to get anywhere.

Focus your mind on energy. Breathe that energy deep into your lungs, taste it in your mouth. Then use that energy to power purposeful activity.

a. Depression and lack of energy

Lack of energy is very often due to emotional problems. While poor diet and habitual inactivity make matters worse, one of the most important reasons for feeling tired all the time is unhappiness. If you are unable to resolve problems at home or at work, when you feel bad, lonely or unwanted, you may feel too tired to do anything.

What can you do? First, establish your own personal list of priorities. Start looking after your own needs, stop worrying about others. Life is worthless when you are unable to enjoy it – so look for ways you can increase the pleasure content of your own life. Break out of the ties that hold you; forget duty and responsibility for a while. Take a holiday if you can, look at your life from a new perspective. You will function better in every way when you've resolved the problems that preoccupy you.

Look for help if you cannot work things out on your own. Consult a counsellor or a psychologist, or the alternative therapist of your choice. Some doctors can be very helpful, if they're willing to devote time to listening to people with emotional problems, rather than just prescribing a short-term palliative. Or perhaps you've heard of a healer in your locality. Don't leave any stone unturned until you are functioning properly. Don't be embarrassed to ask for help: we all need it at times. Nor should you imagine your problems are too trivial; the most seriously depressed people characteristically start their therapeutic interviews by suggesting that their need is so minor, they shouldn't be wasting the therapist's time.

When the mind is down, working on your body will rebalance your emotions. So take care to eat right and make sure you go outdoors every day; at the least, take a walk or cycle ride. Your mind will work better when your body's working better; the brain needs good nutrition and plenty of oxygen. Jogging in the open air is now a recognised therapy for depression – and it works better than drugs! Start building the positive cycle with the basic essentials for a healthy life.

11. Pregnancy

The EAT YOURSELF THIN system will keep you healthy throughout pregnancy and ensure the best possible chance for your baby. Exercise during pregnancy is likely to make the birth easier because you'll be fitter and in better condition. However you will have to keep the intensity of exercise well within your personal capacity, and you may not want to continue with the same types of exercise as you grow bigger. You may have to give up active sports such as squash but find that swimming, when your weight is supported, remains enjoyable. The Long Haul track is best during pregnancy and for at least 2 months after the birth.

Many women have been made over-anxious about weight gain during pregnancy. It has been fashionable, especially in the United States, for women to try to limit weight gain by restricting food intake. This is a very foolish strategy for which there is no convincing medical or physiological justification. In fact, women who start pregnancy plumper than the experts recommend and who put on substantial weight during pregnancy are statistically more likely to have healthy babies. But the weight you gain should be quality flesh, both yours and your baby's, sustained by plenty of nutritious food and maintained by regular continuous activity.

12. Breastfeeding

Women lose fat naturally during breastfeeding. It is a very beneficial process for both mother and baby which gets your muscles back in shape and protects your baby from illness. Continue to eat well, as much as you want, keeping to the dietary guidelines described in Chapter Five.

Do not make any deliberate attempts to shed fat by increasing your activity level substantially when you are breastfeeding. The Long Haul track should provide as much activity as you require. If you are burning off too much fat, your milk may be loaded with toxins from your fat stores and your baby will suffer. Regular activity such as gentle cycling and a daily walk will keep you in shape and maintain those fat-burning systems so that they will be ready to fire up as soon as you intensify your activity regime.

CHAPTER 12

Enjoying Success

IN CHAPTER ONE we asked you to imagine that your problem was that you were getting too thin. By now, even if you have not started to EAT YOURSELF THIN, you should see how this is entirely possible.

Using food to raise your metabolic rate so that you can shed fat gives you control over your body. Training your muscles to burn fat not only keeps you thin, but allows you to extend your control to be a physically competent person. And in its turn physical control extends your mental abilities, enabling you to use your capacity to greater advantage.

Can this train of events really have been initiated just by eating more food? Certainly, by eating enough of the right sort of food you have changed your body and yourself. By becoming active you have changed the detailed physiology of your body make-up, as well as re-shaping it nearer to your heart's desire.

But you have done much more than this. You have laid the foundation for sound health for the rest of your life. The activities you use to train your muscles to burn fat and to shed the surplus you were carrying will have given you a healthy cardiovascular system and increased your liver's capacity to protect you from environmental hazards. Becoming physical will also have increased your confidence; you will know that you will be more capable in any unforeseen situation.

Those people who remain slim, fit and attractive well into old age are those whose lifestyle meets their individual needs. The advice we give in this book on the relevance of diet, pure fresh air, activity balanced by rest, and self-knowledge and respect, is based on universal truths for the health of our species. Whether you are interested in health or not, it will be intuitively obvious that you will benefit from a lifestyle that is designed to fit your personal requirements.

Changing from being a fat person to a thin one can be like travelling to another country. Although you will still be you, everything will have changed in subtle ways, much as things are the same yet different in foreign places. Sensible preparation can help you avoid culture shock when you travel and the same applies to the transition from fat to thin.

You may have to think about new clothes, not just because your shape has changed but because your old clothes no longer suit your feelings and lifestyle. Big people are restricted in their choice of clothes; many lose interest, going for a plain and self-effacing shape disguise. As you change, your clothes will change. Go for things that make positive statements which complement your new lifestyle. Do not be put off by those around who were accustomed to the old you.

The new active you will need clothes that match a more active lifestyle, and it is likely that these will be younger styles. Fashion is moving in your favour with soft, stretchy fabrics and styles created for active people. Now you are used to looking at yourself in the mirror, you will be in a much better position to judge what is right for you. And your experience of being active will enable you to assess the right sorts of garment for the way you live. If you yearn to wear jeans, but shy away and hide in tent-like dresses, your changing priorities will encourage you to put on the clothes that make movement enjoyable. Instead of wearing high heels every day to disguise a dumpy silhouette, you will be choosing comfortable shoes which allow you to walk whenever you fancy, to get on your bike or even jump with joy! The old restrictions on choice and movement are part of the nightmare of the past.

The same is true of other areas of life of particular interest to women. Perhaps you relied on a good face make-up job as a way of compensating for the rest of your appearance. EATING YOURSELF THIN gives you an inner glow that will allow you to use make-up as part of your message to the world rather than as protective camouflage against it.

Now you are enjoying the success of EATING YOURSELF THIN, the perspective of your use of both clothes and make-up will have changed. Instead of seeing them as a means hiding that of which you felt was unattractive – a negative attitude – you will now be able to concentrate on using them to enhance and augment something you have every right to be proud of: a much more positive use of the opportunities clothes and make-up offer.

We have observed a paradox in these things which might affect you. It is that when you are healthy, your skin fresh and smooth and your eyes naturally bright, the superficialities of clothes and make-up seem to be less important. With an inner confidence born of physical competence and radiant beauty more than skin deep, *you* become your statement to the world. You do not need paint and perfume to do it for you.

Whichever way your inclinations lead you, there is no doubt that you will enjoy the biggest boost to attractiveness that EATING YOURSELF THIN will bring. No matter what they wear, there is no doubt that most people are at their most attractive when they *feel* attractive. Your new diet and active lifestyle should certainly make you feel good, and as your confidence grows, so will your feeling of being attractive.

Whatever accompanies your change in shape and lifestyle, you will find people react differently to you. This is to be expected because you *are* different. Changing your inner picture of yourself, despite growing accustomed to your shape in the mirror, may take more time. You may find yourself being caught off-guard and behaving as the old hesitant you, rather than the positive new you. It may be a little bit like growing up again, you make silly mistakes and sometimes get embarrassed until you adjust your inner picture to the new outer reality. This can be an enjoyable experience;

your past will have given you wisdom to guard against excesses, while the new you will be able selectively to open doors on new aspects of life.

Success is based upon the recognition that we have no alternative but to work with our bodies. By fulfilling the body's needs you enable it to fulfil yours. You live as the integrated being you are, at peace within and gaining pleasure from yourself. The energy which is locked into the dieter's perpetual struggle has been liberated for positive use in living, in enjoying life. The strength you draw from the balanced lifestyle you have created puts you in the position to go on to whatever you wish in fulfilling your unique personal potential.

Pleasure in your new self may make you wish to aim for your idea of perfection. You may find that you like certain styles of clothes, or shapes of bodies, and wish to be more like that yourself. There is no reason why you should not. Your need for maintenance activity to keep your metabolic rate up could be satisfied by selective muscle building or refining to reshape those parts of you which will benefit from it. The principles were explained earlier, and if you have been using weight-training to burn fat, you will have a good idea of what is needed. Working on yourself in this way can be very rewarding, as any body builder (or body refiner) will tell you. If you haven't been doing weight-training this could be the time to start.

It may be that you have become hooked on your performance rather than your shape. Sports, either competitive or just pleasurable, will be your answer. We know ex-dieters, now slim, who use their desire for an outstanding fortnight on the ski slopes to keep them active for the rest of the year. They may be extreme, but the less single-minded still find a reason to keep fit in a variety of sports. Whatever you do, even the mundane everyday chores, is more enjoyable if you are fit enough to make the most of what life has to offer.

It is very important to see life in this positive way. You are likely to find that in working on your body you also improve your mind. There is nothing strange or mysterious about this; the reason why animals have brains is to control and coordinate complicated movements. In becoming more physically competent, you will inevitably become more mentally competent. The good food you are eating will help this process, as will your ability to oxygenate your body. It may be that you find yourself putting activity on to a maintenance routine, and using your new energy for other interests. Go with it, follow anything which takes your interest, whether a qualification or a hobby; there is the Open University, for example, as well as many other opportunities. The world (as they used to say) is your oyster.

Next time you see yourself in the mirror, take a moment to see if there isn't something else there that may have been absent in the past. One of the effects of becoming lean and competent and feeling your confidence grow as you achieve the goals you have set yourself will be the emergence of self-respect. Understanding how your body works, how to select food and activity to fulfil your needs, and feeling the positive response that using this understanding brings can only lead to this. The dieter, always searching for the miracle, and always failing, has no chance of ever coming to terms with self in this positive way. In the long run this may be your greatest source of pleasure in your success.

In creating a dynamic balance in your life founded on understanding and respect, many of the old things which preoccupied your life are no longer relevant. The old food obsession, the constant battle with self and hunger, the continual anxiety about food and fat, have all been banished. Being in balance means you are in a position of strength. While others struggle with illusions and grapple with phantoms of success, you have succeeded; you are the object of their envy.

From this position of strength you can go on, to wherever energy, ambition or desire lead you.

Menus

THE THREE MENUS in this Appendix are guides to the sorts of foods you should choose, and the sort of quantities that we anticipate you will need. There is no need to stick rigidly to our suggestions: you are not on a slimming diet but developing a style of eating that will suit you for the rest of your life. As you grow more confident, you will want to add the particular types of food you prefer, but remember always to go for quality.

Our choices are based on the dietary guidelines described in Chapters Six and Seven; the aim is to keep your intake of animal and processed fats low, complex carbohydrates high, and to eat whenever you wish. We have made the evening meal the largest but you should feel free to swap lunch and dinner menus if you prefer to eat more earlier in the day.

Menu 1: Moderate energy intake

This level of consumption would be appropriate for a previously sedentary man just starting to EAT HIMSELF THIN, for a woman starting on the Fast Track or after Week 3 of the Happy Medium Action Plan. When you are not working hard to EAT YOURSELF THIN, it may be sufficient for maintenance, but you must eat more if you feel hungry. Miss whatever snacks you don't feel you need but never have fewer than three meals a day.

Breakfast
$\frac{1}{4}$ pt fresh orange juice mixed 50:50 with sparkling water
   or fresh grapefruit
3 oz sugar-free muesli with skimmed milk/yoghurt and
   fresh fruit

or wholewheat cereal with skimmed milk
or porridge (no sugar)
2 slices toast, thinly buttered
  or 1 egg and 1 slice toast
Herb tea – we recommend rosehip

Elevenses
1 slice toast or 3 rice cakes with banana
Diluted fruit juice, tea, coffee or herb tea

Lunch
Large baked potato with beans, tuna or a little grated
  cheese
  or wholemeal pasta with tomato sauce and side salad
  or wholemeal pitta filled with beans and salad
  or split pea and vegetable soup with wholemeal rolls
Fresh fruit
Mineral water

Tea
Egg, fish or salad sandwich
Tea

Dinner
Avocado vinaigrette
  or fresh grapefruit
  or crudités
  or fresh vegetable soup
Fresh baked fish with potatoes and green vegetables
  or nutroast with lightly tossed salad and organic brown
    rice
  or roast turkey with plenty of vegetables and potato
  or tandoori chicken/lamb with rice, salad and raita
  or rabbit/game casserole with vegetables
Fresh fruit with natural yoghurt or quark
Lemon verbena or peppermint tea

Evening snacks
Apple/orange or other fresh fruit
Rice cakes
Brazils, almonds, walnuts or cashew nuts

Menu 2: Minimal energy intake

This menu is suitable for a woman just starting to EAT HERSELF THIN, or people on the Long Haul whose activity level remains relatively low. You will need to eat more than this when your activity level has risen on the Happy Medium or Fast Track. It delivers about 2,000 to 2,300 calories.

Breakfast
$\frac{1}{8}$ pt orange juice mixed 50:50 with natural mineral water
   or fresh grapefruit (no sugar)
2 oz sugar-free muesli with skimmed milk/yoghurt
   or wholewheat cereal with skimmed milk
   or porridge (no sugar)
1 egg
1 slice toast
Herb tea – we recommend rosehip

Elevenses
2 rice cakes
Diluted fruit juice, tea, coffee or herb tea

Lunch
Lightly tossed salad with organic brown rice, sprinkled with sunflower seed
   or wholemeal pitta filled with salad
   or baked potato with tuna
Fresh fruit
Mineral water

Tea
Cucumber, tomato or salad sandwich
Tea

Dinner
Melon, grapefruit or fresh fruit juice
Fresh trout, salmon or herring with peas, carrots, baked potato
   or walnut and avocado salad with potato
   or 2 eggs, salad and rice or potato
   or pasta with tuna/seafood sauce and salad

or vegetarian bean moussaka
    or tandoori chicken with rice and salad
Fresh fruit salad with natural yoghurt or quark
Lemon verbena or peppermint tea

Evening snack
Apple or other fresh fruit
2 rice cakes

Menu 3: High-energy diet

This menu is suitable for women on the Fast Track, or
    after Week 4 of Happy Medium. Men starting to EAT
    THEMSELVES THIN will find it sufficient while their
    activity level is relatively low but you may want to
    eat more when you are established on the Happy
    Medium or Fast Track. It delivers about 3,000 cal-
    ories.

Breakfast
$\frac{1}{4}$ pt fresh orange juice mixed 50:50 with sparkling water
    or fresh grapefruit
    or stewed figs or prunes with natural yoghurt
Plate of porridge
    or 3 oz sugar-free muesli with skimmed milk/yoghurt
    or wholewheat cereal with skimmed milk
1 egg
Wholemeal bread – as much as you want
Herb tea – we recommend rosehip

Elevenses
Toast or rice cakes with nut butter and banana
Tea, coffee or herb tea

Lunch
Large baked potato with tuna salad
    or pitta with beans and salad
    or pasta with tuna/seafood sauce and salad
    or vegetarian moussaka
    or fish or low-fat cheese and salad sandwiches
Fresh fruit
Mineral water

Tea
Large cheese and tomato sandwich
Fresh fruit
Tea or fruit juice and mineral water

Dinner
$\frac{1}{2}$ grapefruit or melon (no sugar)
   or fresh fruit juice
   or avocado vinaigrette
   or lentil, pea, or potato and leek soup
Lean meat roast
   or meat or bean casserole
   or stew
   or fish
   or nutroast with vegetables and potatoes, pasta or rice
   or omelette with lightly tossed salad or peas and potato
Fresh fruit salad
   or baked apple
   or boiled wild (hunza) apricots with natural yoghurt
     or quark
Lemon verbena or peppermint tea

Evening snacks
Apple or other fresh fruit
Rice cakes
Mixed nuts, figs and raisins
Natural yoghurt with fresh fruit and wheatgerm

EYT Basic Breathing, Mobility and Floor Exercises

1. Breathing

Our basic breathing routine takes about 2 minutes. If you use it regularly you will soon find yourself breathing more deeply most of the time, and you will slip into a deeper way of breathing automatically when the need arises.

Start sitting upright on an ordinary chair with your knees slightly apart. As you breathe out, slide your hands down your thighs in between your knees as if you were going to touch your toes. Let your shoulders go down towards your knees, so that your ribs are compressed, and as much air as possible is squeezed out.

Then breathe in, pulling your shoulders back and straightening your spine. Keep pulling air in until your chest is full and your ribs are as high as they will go.

Hold your breath for a steady count of four – count 'one and two and three and four' in your head, then *slowly* breathe out without changing your posture.

Remain in the same position and breathe in and out as slowly, deeply, and rhythmically as you can for 4 deep breaths. Then repeat from the beginning.

Go through the complete cycle 6 times, concentrating on getting as much air in and out as you can. Closing your eyes may help.

Do not worry if you feel slightly dizzy (but breathe more quickly until you recover!); that is the effect of unaccustomed oxygen levels. You will soon get used to it. Nor should you worry if your heart pounds as you rise up and breathe in. You have taken a load off it and should try to keep it off with a consistently relaxed upright posture.

When you have mastered this routine, you can add another part. Make sure you are not wearing restrictive clothing and breathe as you do when asleep, using your diaphragm. This will strengthen its action and give you more control during vigorous activity.

When you have straightened up and slowly exhaled, allowing your chest to subside, breathe in again by pushing your stomach out. Do not allow your chest to rise. Exhale by drawing your stomach in again. Breathe by raising and lowering your chest, and alternatively with your diaphragm by pushing in and out with your stomach – it is your diaphragm that does the pushing and pulling. Alternating in this way will make you breathe consciously, slowly and deeply.

To really fill yourself up with air, you can combine both movements. When you have exhaled with your ribs right up, hold them there; breathe in again until your chest is full, and then draw in more air by pushing your stomach out. Breathe out by reversing the process, as slowly as you can. This will really super-charge your system.

2. Mobility

This section is intended for those whose range of movement and ability may be severely restricted.

We want to encourage you to extend your range of movement while you are changing your eating patterns. You should ensure that you do the breathing routine above at least 4 times a day – or even more often.

The movements below will lead into the floor exercises listed after them; they are designed to increase progressively the use of muscle groups you are probably neglecting. Your underlying problem is probably not that your major muscle groups are undeveloped, but that fat prevents you from using them effectively. Take heart; a little detour will initiate the solution, and although you will have to take a longer route, you will arrive in the end.

Do not underestimate the demands you may be putting on yourself; prepare properly, wear looser clothing, and have some soft and easy music if you feel it will help. Take your time and enjoy the sensation of movement.

Mobility movements
After the breathing routine, go through the following movements. Keep the chair handy, you will need it again.

1. Stand comfortably with your feet a foot or so apart and your arms loosely by your sides; keep your back straight and your shoulders back. Now just bend your knees a little so that you sink down a few inches. You must judge how far you can manage. Then swing your arms up in front and above your head and reach up as far as you can; as you swing up, straighten your legs and rise up on your toes. Breathe in as you reach up, out as you lower your arms slowly to your sides again. Repeat 6 times, linking the movements continuously and timing them to match your natural breathing.

You could break this movement into two if necessary, by sitting and raising your arms and stretching up, then standing and doing the leg movement using the back of your chair for support.

2. Either seating or standing, lift your arms out to the sides until they are level with your shoulders. Stretch out as far as you can with your fingertips. Now slowly move your straight arms so that your fingertips go round in small circles, breathing in as they go up and back, and out as they go down and forwards. Take your timing from your natural breathing. Once you have got the rhythm, gradually increase the size of the circles until they are as big as you can make them. You may prefer to start by letting your arms hang loosely at your sides, and shrugging your shoulders into circles; if you do, keep your breathing and timing the same.

3. Stand behind your chair so you can use the back as a support. Stand with your legs comfortably apart and bend forward from the waist, with your legs and back straight, so that your back is parallel to the floor like an ironing board. Use your hands on the back of the chair for support and to help you straighten up again. Do not worry if you cannot make a perfect shape. *Feel* the effort of straightening up in the back of your thighs and buttocks and try to keep your back straight throughout. Breathe out going down, and in coming up. Do it 8 times if you can. Slow and easy, in time with your breathing.

4. Lie on your back; a firm surface with a soft covering is best. Place your arms by your sides, feet a little apart. One leg at a time, bring your knee up until your thigh is pointing straight up. Don't try to keep your leg straight, just let your foot dangle. Then lower your knee and straighten out your leg. Repeat with the other leg. Breathe in as you raise, out as you lower. If that is easy for 8 times on each leg, start straightening your leg once your knee is raised, and lower your leg in the straight position.

5. Same position. Stretch your arms straight up so your fingers point to the ceiling. Keeping your arms straight, lower them backwards; then sweep them round so they are straight out from your shoulders; then raise them to the original position. Breathe in as you lower, hold as you sweep round, and out as you raise. As you do a dozen easy movements, concentrate on feeling the muscles that are moving your arms.

Then up and out for a walk. As long as you can manage.

3. Floor Exercises

The following exercises are used to make up three schedules, A, B, and C. Some of the movements have three options; short, for beginners; intermediate, for most general use, and long, mainly for those on Fast Track. Use whichever suits your particular ability.

Use your notebook to note your particular routine. This will be useful practice if you intend to go on to a gym or to do weight-training; you will need to keep track of poundages, repetitions and other such things. It is also a useful way of recording your progress.

Schedule A is a basic routine, consisting of movements which in their short form are suitable for beginners. Many of these can be extended to suit intermediates, so that beginners will naturally progress as their ability increases.

Schedule B is a good general purpose workout; many movements are the same as Schedule A but in more advanced form. The additional movements in this schedule are also progressive.

Schedule C consists of movements which make a good general purpose warm-up routine. This should be used before going on to other more strenuous activity. It can also be used as a daily maintenance routine when other activity is not possible.

When starting any schedule you should select the form of movement, i.e. short, intermediate or long, which is well within your capacity. Once you can cope easily with *the whole schedule* try the more extended forms, starting with the exercises you find most difficult. When you have reached the final form of all movements, speed up!

If you start on Schedule A, try the extra movements in B when you feel ready. If you can manage them without strain, change to B.

Schedule C is for warming up prior to other activity. Do each movement until you begin to feel the strain; do not push yourself to your limit.

Whichever schedule you follow, it is a good idea to go through the basic breathing routine first (see page 167).

Schedule A movements

1. ARM SWINGS

SHORT
- Position: standing legs naturally apart, arms by sides.
- Movement: raise arms to the front and swing up and back in the largest circle you can make, moving continuously.
- Breathing: in as arms rise, out as they descend.
- Style: aim for easy continuous movement, do not jerk or shake your body.
- Duration: at least 30 seconds (around 20 circles).

2. ARM RAISES

SHORT
- Position: standing, arms straight by side.
- Movement: raise arms to each side, twisting to clap hands lightly over head, arms straight all the time, and lower.
- Breathing: in as arms rise, out as lowered.
- Style: aim for an easy rhythmical swing, reaching up as high as you can.
- Duration: continue for at least 30 seconds (roughly 14 to 20 movements).

INTERMEDIATE
- Position: standing, legs naturally together.
- Movement: arms as Short, as arms are raised, jump legs apart, starting with a small distance between feet and increasing with ability. Return jump as arms are lowered.
- Breathing: as for short form.
- Style: as Short; aim for continuous movement, do not stop between jumps. To increase effect, increase speed; but maintain rhythmic breathing.
- Duration: as required.

3. TOUCHING TOES

SHORT
- Position: stand upright, hands by side, legs slightly apart.

- Movement: bend forward from hips and waist, keeping legs straight (rise up on toes if it helps), continue until you touch your toes (or as near as you can manage), return to upright, using arms and chair if necessary.
- Breathing: out as you bend over, in as you straighten up.
- Style: deliberate movement; bend forward, pause, straighten, pause, repeat.
- Duration: 10 to 20 movements.

INTERMEDIATE
- Position: as Short.
- Movement: as Short, but once touching toes (or nearly), rise a few inches and press down at them again; repeat so that you touch 4 times while continuing to exhale.
- Breathing: as Short, but deeper.
- Style: an easier swing.
- Duration: as Short.

LONG
- Position: start as Short.
- Movement: swing arms up above head before swinging down to touch toes. Continue as Intermediate.
- Breathing: in as arms are swung up, otherwise as Intermediate.
- Style: a continuous easy swing.
- Duration: as Short.

4. KNEE RAISES

SHORT
- Position: standing, using chairback for support if desired.
- Movement: raise knee as high as possible while keeping back straight.
- Breathing: in as knee is raised, out as lowered.
- Style: an easy continuous movement; use your breathing to time it.
- Duration: 10 to 20 movements each leg.

INTERMEDIATE

- Position: as Short.
- Movement: as Short, but when knee is at maximum height straighten leg.
- Breathing: as Short.
- Style: more like a dance movement.
- Duration: as Short.

LONG

- Position: as Short.
- Movement: more of a dancer's high kick but do not lose the knee-bend movement.
- Breathing: as Short.
- Style: definite dance.
- Duration: as Short.

5. PRESS UPS

SHORT

- Position: stand facing a wall, reach out with both arms straight just below shoulder height. Lean forward until you are supported by the wall with the palms of your hands flat against the wall.
- Movement: keeping your legs and back straight, sink towards the wall, then push away again until your arms are straight. Repeat.
- Breathing: out as you sink to the wall, in as you push away.
- Style: positive and purposeful.
- Duration: adjust your distance from the wall so that you can do at least 8 movements. When you can do 12 standing so that your outstretched arms are a foot away from the wall before you begin, move on to Intermediate.

INTERMEDIATE

- Position: lying face down on floor, palms flat on floor under shoulders.
- Movement: keeping back straight, but bending at the knees, push up until your arms are straight; lower and repeat.

- Breathing: in as you push up, out as you lower.
- Style: determined.
- Duration: build up to 12, then go on to Long.

LONG
- Position: as Intermediate.
- Movement: as Intermediate, but do not bend at the knees.
- Breathing: as Intermediate.
- Style: as Intermediate.
- Duration: up to 12 movements.

6. CALF RAISES

SHORT
- Position: stand facing wall or supporting yourself with a chairback.
- Movement: raise yourself as high as possible on the balls of your feet, and lower.
- Breathing: freely.
- Style: purposeful; move easily without jerking.
- Duration: until the effort starts to strain.

INTERMEDIATE
- Position: as Short, but with balls (front) of feet raised 1 to 2 inches on a piece of wood. A book will not take the strain.
- Movement: start with heels on the ground, then raise yourself as in Short.
- Breathing: as in Short.
- Style: as in Short.
- Duration: as in Short.

LONG
- Position: as Intermediate.
- Movement: as Intermediate, but when you have stretched up as high as you can go, try to tense the muscles in your thighs, buttocks, back and shoulders, working progressively up your body. Then relax and lower. Stop tensing at the first sign of cramp.
- Breathing: in as you rise and tense.
- Style: more purposeful.
- Duration: until you feel it.

7. LEG RAISES

SHORT
- Position: lying on back, arms by sides.
- Movement: keeping your legs straight, first raise your right foot about 1 foot in the air, and lower. Repeat for left leg.
- Breathing: out as you raise, in as you lower.
- Style: slow and easy, aim for continuous movement.
- Duration: up to 12 each leg, then move on to Intermediate.

INTERMEDIATE
- Position: as Short.
- Movement: keeping legs straight, raise both together until your toes are pointing to the ceiling, lower and repeat.
- Breathing: as Short.
- Style: slow and easy, avoid jerking your feet up and letting them bang down.
- Duration: up to 12 movements, then move on to Long.

LONG
- Position: as Short.
- Movement: keeping legs straight as far as possible, swing both legs up together and aim to touch the floor behind your head.
- Breathing: as Short.
- Style: more purposeful, taking your timing from your breathing.
- Duration: stop when you can no longer maintain the rhythm with your breathing.

8. SIDE LEG RAISES

SHORT
- Position: lying on your side. Use cushions or other strategic padding if required.
- Movement: raise your upper leg vertically as high as you can, and lower. Repeat. Turn on to your other side and repeat with other leg.

- Breathing: in as you raise, out as you lower.
- Style: light and easy, continuous movement in time with your natural breathing.
- Duration: up to 12 movements each leg, then move on to Intermediate.

INTERMEDIATE
- Position: as Short.
- Movement: raise your leg as high as possible, then point your toes and swing your leg to point the largest circle you can with your toes. Keep rotating until you are tired, then rest.
- Breathing: naturally.
- Duration: repeat as many circles as you can twice for each leg.

9. ARM RAISES

SHORT
- Position: lying flat on your back, arms straight out to sides, level with your shoulders.
- Movement: keeping your arms straight, raise them so your hands meet above your face; lower and repeat.
- Breathing: out as you raise – really push the air out of your chest – and in as you lower, drawing in as much air as you can.
- Style: rhythmic and purposeful.
- Duration: up to 10 movements.

INTERMEDIATE
- Position: as Short.
- Movement: as Short, but try holding some weight in each hand (tins of peas are good for a start; later you might want to buy some weights)
- Breathing: as Short.
- Style: as Short.
- Duration: as Short.

LONG
- Position: as Short, except raise your upper back 6 inches to 1 foot from the floor, either on a firm

cushion or on a short bench. It does not matter if you are higher from the floor, but your back must be well supported.

● Movement: keeping your arms straight, let them sink below your shoulder level between 6 inches and 1 foot before raising them as before. Use weights as required.

● Breathing: as Short.

● Style: as Short.

● Duration: as Short.

That concludes Schedule A. When you have finished it, allow a few minutes to shake yourself out or dance to loosen up all over.

Schedule B movements

Note: some movements have alternatives; select according to your build and ability.

1. as Schedule A

3. as Schedule A

4. as Schedule A if you are of heavy build

Otherwise:

10. SQUATS

SHORT

● Position: standing, legs slightly apart. You might find it helpful to raise your heels on a wooden block 1 inch to $1\frac{1}{2}$ inches thick (you can get away with a book for this one).

● Movement: keeping your back as straight as possible, bend your knees and sink down into a squat, pause, and rise up to your original position. Repeat.

● Breathing: out as you sink, in as you rise.

● Style: rhythmical, in time with your breathing. Do not try to go fast.

● Duration: up to 25 movements.

LONG
- Position: as Short, but without block under heels.
- Movement: as Short, but much more dynamic; as you rise, project yourself up into the air, throw your arms up to reach as high as you can before you land and sink back into the squat. Repeat.
- Breathing: in as you jump up, out as you sink.
- Style: continuous movement.
- Duration: up to 12 movements.

7. as Schedule A

8. as Schedule A

If you are of light build:

11. HEADS AND HEELS

SHORT
- Position: lying face-down on a firm surface, arms straight, hands just under thighs, legs slightly apart.
- Movement: keeping your legs as straight as you can, arch your back, raise your legs and pull your shoulders back, lifting your head as high as you can – so that you form a banana shape balanced on your hips. Return to original position. Try to feel your thighs lifting off your hands.
- Breathing: in as you arch, out as you relax.
- Style: this one always feels awkward; try to pull your back tight as you arch, but do not hold it, relax immediately. It should be a fairly rapid movement but start slowly until you are sure you have got it right.
- Duration: between 10 and 20 movements.

LONG
- Position: as Short, except arms straight out above head.
- Movement: basically as Short, but as you arch, your legs and arms open so that you form an X.
- Breathing: as Short.
- Style: as Short.
- Duration: as Short.

If you are of medium or heavy build:

12. ALTERNATE TOE TOUCHING

- Position: legs apart and straight, bend forward at waist keeping your back straight, try to get your back parallel to the floor, then arms out straight level with your shoulders.
- Movement: keep your arms and shoulders more or less in the same position; twist your trunk at the waist and touch your left foot with your right hand, then twist your trunk the other way and touch your right foot with your left hand. Repeat.
- Breathing: slightly awkward for this movement; you will find you can breathe in easily while twisting, but you may have to make a conscious effort to breathe out. Breathe in while twisting one way and out when twisting the other.
- Style: an easy, swinging continuous movement.
- Duration: until breathless.

9. as Schedule A

13. SIT UPS

SHORT
- Position: lying flat on your back, legs together, arms by sides. It might be helpful to hook your feet under a bed or sofa to hold them down.
- Movement: keeping your legs and back as straight as possible, bend at the waist until you are sitting upright. Keeping legs and back straight, lower to original position.
- Breathing: out as you sit up, in as you lower.
- Style: as brisk as possible.
- Duration: up to 20 movements.

INTERMEDIATE
- Position: as Short, but arms straight out above head; keep them in this position throughout the movement.
- Movement: as Short.

- Breathing: as Short.
- Style: as Short.
- Duration: as Short.

LONG
- Position: as Short.
- Movement: as Intermediate, but swing right through and touch your toes.
- Breathing: as Short.
- Style: as Short.
- Duration: as Short.

5. as Schedule A

Finish up by 10 to 15 minutes running/jogging, or skipping, or very energetic dance.

Schedule C movements: Warm up or Maintenance

1. as Schedule A

3. as Schedule A

10. Short, as Schedule B

11. (either option), as Schedule B

5. as Schedule A

2. Intermediate, as Schedule A

A little running or skipping will bring your system up so you are ready for something strenuous like rowing or weight-training; keep the effort low so that you remain warm but do not become breathless.

Further Reading

BODY, R. *Red or Green for Farmers (and the rest of us)*, Saffron Walden, Broad Leys Publishing, 1987.

DAVIES, S. AND STEWART, A. *Nutritional Medicine*, London, Pan Books, 1987.

ELKINGTON, J. AND HAILES, J. *The Green Consumer Guide*, London, Gollancz, 1988.

GEAR, A. *The New Organic Food Guide*, London, Dent, 1987.

GIBSON, S., TEMPLETON, L. AND GIBSON, R. *Cook Yourself a Favour*, Northampton, Thorsons, 1986.

KENTON, L. AND KENTON, S. *Raw Energy*, London, Century, 1984.

MELVILLE, A. AND JOHNSON, C. *Persistent Fat and How to Lose It*, London, Century, 1985.

MELVILLE, A. AND JOHNSON, C. *Alternatives to Drugs*, London, Fontana, 1987.

MELVILLE, A. AND JOHNSON, C. *The Complete Diet Book*, London, Grafton, 1989.

MANSFIELD, P. AND MONRO, J. *Chemical Children: How to Protect Your Family from Harmful Pollutants*, London, Century, 1987.

YUDKIN, J. *Pure, White and Deadly*, London, Davis-Poynter, 1972.

References

ADAM, K. AND OSWALD, M. 'Sleep helps healing', *British Medical Journal*, November 1984, 1400–1.

ASTRAND, P. O. 'Diet, Performance, and their Interaction', in Barker, L. M. (ed.), *The Psychobiology of Human Food Selection*, Westport, Conn: Avi, 1982.

ASTRAND, P. O. AND RODAHL, K. *Textbook of Work Physiology*, New York, McGraw-Hill, 1977.

BELLER, A. S. *Fat and Thin*, New York, Farrar, Straus & Giroux, 1977.

BJORNTORP, P. 'Physiological and clinical aspects of exercise in obese persons', *Exercise and Sport Sciences Reviews*, 11, 1983, 159–80.

BLAND, J. *Medical Applications of Clinical Nutrition*, New Canaan, Keats, 1985.

BODY, R. *Red or Green for Farmers (and the rest of us)*, Saffron Walden, Broad Leys Publishing, 1987.

BROOKS, G. A. AND FAHEY, T. D. *Exercise Physiology*, New York, Wiley, 1984.

BROWNELL, K. D. AND STUNKARD, A. J. 'Physical activity in the development and control of obesity', in Stunkard, A. (ed.), *Obesity*, Philadelphia, W. B. Saunders, 1980.

BRUCH, H. *Eating Disorders: Obesity, anorexia nervosa and the person within*, London, Routledge & Kegan Paul, 1974.

BRYCE-SMITH, D. AND HODGKINSON, L. *The Zinc Solution*, London, Century, 1986.

CAMPBELL, W. W. AND ANDERSON, R. A. 'Effects of aerobic exercise and training on the trace minerals chromium, zinc and copper', *Sports Medicine*, 4, 1987, 9–18.

COSTILL, D. *A Scientific Approach to Distance Running*, New York, Track and Field News, 1979.

DAVIES, S. AND STEWART, A. *Nutritional Medicine*, London, Pan Books, 1987.

FELIG, P. 'Effects of exercise and physical training on field utilization, insulin sensitivity, and insulin secretion', in Borer, K. T., *et al.* (eds.), *Frontiers of Exercise Biology*, Champaign, Ill., Human Kinetics Publishers Inc., 1983.

FORBES, G. B. *Human Body Composition*, New York, Springer-Verlag, 1987.

GARROW, J. S. *Energy Balance and Obesity in Man*, Amsterdam, Elsevier, 1978.

LAMB, D. *Physiology of Exercise*, New York, Macmillan, 1978.

MAUGHAN, R. J., *et al.* 'Fat and carbohydrate metabolism during low intensity exercise: effects of the availability of muscle glycogen', *European Journal of Applied Physiology*, 1978, 7–17.

MELVILLE, A. AND JOHNSON, C. *Persistent Fat and How to Lose It*, London, Century, 1985.

   Alternatives to Drugs, London, Fontana, 1987.

   The Complete Diet Book, London, Grafton, 1989.

MUTRIE, N. The psychological benefits of exercise for women, in Borer, K. T., *et al.* (eds.), *Frontiers of Exercise Biology*, Champaign, Ill., Human Kinetics Publishers Inc., 1983.

NEWSHOLME, E. AND LEECH, T. *The Runner*, Roosevelt, N.J., Fitness Books, 1983.

NYGAARD, E. AND HEDE, K. 'Physiological profiles of the male and female', in Macleod, D. *et al.*, *Exercise: Benefits, Limits and Adaptations*, London, E. & F. N. Spon, 1987.

PASSWATER, R. A. AND CRANTON, E. M. *Trace Elements, Hair Analysis and Nutrition*, New Canaan, Keats, 1983.

PAUL, A. A. AND SOUTHGATE, D. A. T. *McCance & Widdowson's The Composition of Foods*, London, HMSO, 1978.

PRE-MENSTRUAL TENSION ADVISORY SERVICE (Lewes, Sussex), *A Study of the British Diet*, 1986.
 Weight loss as a result of the nutritional approach to the pre-menstrual syndrome, 1985.

PRIOR, J. C. 'Exercise-related adaptive changes of the menstrual cycle', in Macleod, D., *et al.*, *Exercise: Benefits, Limits and Adaptations*, London, E. & F. N. Spon, 1987.

RUDIN, D. O. 'Omega-3 essential fatty acids in medicine', *1984–5 Yearbook of Nutritional Medicine*.

STEWART, M. *Beat PMT With Diet*, London, Ebury, 1987.

TROWELL, H. AND BURKITT, D. *Western Diseases: their emergence and prevention*, London, Edward Arnold, 1981.

WYNN, M. AND WYNN, A. *Prevention of Handicap and the Health of Women*, London, Routledge & Kegan Paul, 1979.

INDEX